W9-AAJ-893

Bloom's
GUIDES

Charlotte Brontë's
Jane Eyre

CURRENTLY AVAILABLE

The Adventures of Huckleberry Finn

All the Pretty Horses

Animal Farm

Beloved

Beowulf

Brave New World

The Catcher in the Rye

The Chosen

The Crucible

Cry, the Beloved Country

Death of a Salesman

Fahrenheit 451

Frankenstein

The Glass Menagerie

The Grapes of Wrath

Great Expectations

The Great Gatsby

Hamlet

The Handmaid's Tale

The House on Mango Street

I Know Why the Caged Bird Sings

The Iliad

Jane Eyre

Lord of the Flies

Macbeth

Maggie: A Girl of the Streets

The Member of the Wedding

The Metamorphosis

Native Son

Of Mice and Men

1984

The Odyssey

Oedipus Rex

One Hundred Years of Solitude

Pride and Prejudice

Ragtime

The Red Badge of Courage

Romeo and Juliet

Slaughterhouse-Five

The Scarlet Letter

Snow Falling on Cedars

A Streetcar Named Desire

The Sun Also Rises

A Tale of Two Cities

The Things They Carried

To Kill a Mockingbird

The Waste Land

Bloom's
GUIDES

Charlotte Brontë's
Jane Eyre

Edited & with an Introduction
by Harold Bloom

BLOOM'S
LITERARY CRITICISM
An imprint of Infobase Publishing

Bloom's Guides: Jane Eyre

Copyright © 2007 by Infobase Publishing

Introduction © 2007 by Harold Bloom

Bloom's Literary Criticism
An imprint of Infobase Publishing
132 West 31st Street
New York, NY 10001

Library of Congress Cataloging-in-Publication Data
Charlotte Brontë's Jane Eyre / Harold Bloom, editor.
    p. cm. — (Bloom's guides)
  Includes bibliographical references and index.
  ISBN-13: 978-0-7910-9362-7 (hardcover)
  ISBN-10: 0-7910-9362-X (hardcover)
  1. Brontë, Charlotte, 1816–1855. Jane Eyre. 2. Governesses in literature. I. Bloom, Harold. II. Title: Jane Eyre. III. Series.

  PR4167.J33C43 2007
  823'.8—dc22   2007010024

Contributing Editor: Neil Heims

Cover design by Takeshi Takahashi

Printed in the United States of America

Bang EJB 10 9 8 7 6 5 4 3 2 1

This book is printed on acid-free paper.

Contents

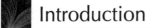
Introduction

HAROLD BLOOM

Charlotte Brontë, particularly in *Jane Eyre*, manifests an aggressivity towards her readers that is infrequent among the major novelists. Though she professed great admiration for William Makepeace Thackeray, the author of *Vanity Fair*, he was not an authentic influence upon her. Like her sister Emily, the poet-novelist who composed *Wuthering Heights*, Charlotte was the perhaps involuntary disciple of the poet Lord Byron, whose personality and works are the inspiration for Rochester in *Jane Eyre* and for Heathcliff in *Wuthering Heights*. Charlotte's vengeance upon Byron is enacted both against her male readers and against Rochester. Byronic dramatization gives us not only Rochester, a pure type of the Byronic hero, but also "the Byronic pride and passion of Jane herself," in the words of the feminist critics Sandra M. Gilbert and Susan Gubar. The sexual intensity of Rochester is matched by that of Jane, whose relation to Rochester is a barely idealized version of Charlotte Brontë's permanent obsession with Lord Byron, who was at once the Ernest Hemingway and the Clark Gable of the Romantic era.

Rochester is all but castrated by Charlotte, since his maiming and blinding by the plot is so curiously gratuitous. If Gustave Flaubert can be said to murder Emma Bovary, while protesting that he is the lady, then it is perhaps true that Charlotte Brontë symbolically castrates Rochester, in the process of taming him into a mate suitable for Jane Eyre. As narrator, Jane scarcely can be distinguished from Charlotte, both sharing the same ferocity of will. The domestication of Rochester, while painful, is less spiritually sadistic than is his religious conversion, a kind of final indignity visited upon Byron's surrogate by the clergyman's daughter, Charlotte Brontë.

The critic Sylvère Monod observed that "Charlotte Brontë is thus led to bully her reader because she distrusts him."

Substitute "Rochester" for "her reader" in that sentence, and it would be just as accurate. When the novel concludes, famously, by telling us: "Reader, I married him," it goes on to give us a peculiarly phrased idealization of the union of Jane Eyre and her battered husband:

> I have now been married ten years. I know what it is to live entirely for and with what I love best on earth. I hold myself supremely blest—blest beyond what language can express; because I am my husband's life as fully as he is mine. No woman was ever nearer to her mate than I am: absolutely more bone of his bone, and flesh of his flesh. I know no weariness of my Edward's society: he knows none of mine, any more than we do of the pulsation of the heart that beats in our separate bosoms; consequently, we are ever together. To be together is for us to be at once as free as in solitude, as gay as in company. We talk, I believe, all day long: to talk to each other is but an animated and audible thinking. All my confidence is bestowed on him; all his confidence is devoted to me: we are precisely suited in character; perfect concord is the result.

This is a radical new version of Adam and Eve: "bone of his bone, and flesh of his flesh." That "perfect concord" is more a total fusion than it is a harmony. We are reminded of Catherine Earnshaw's fierceness in *Wuthering Heights*: "I *am* Heathcliff." A marriage that is almost an ingestion defies the truth that even the most authentic eros unites only in act, not in essence. The drive, the will-to-power over life and the reader, is so consistently maintained by Charlotte Brontë that we do not resist her. Aesthetically, we have our reward, even if her heroine's triumph makes some male readers more than a little uneasy.

Biographical Sketch

Charlotte Brontë was born in Thornton, Yorkshire, in the north of England, in 1816, where her father Patrick was curate, the parish priest. Her mother, Mary Branwell, died in 1821. Brontë was one of six children, five girls and a boy. The two elder sisters, Mary and Elizabeth, died in 1825 of tuberculosis they contracted at school. Charlotte and her sister, Emily Brontë, author of *Wuthering Heights*, also attended the Clergy Daughters' School, an unwholesome and harsh place that became the model for Lowood Institution in *Jane Eyre*. Brontë's third surviving sister, Anne, wrote *Agnes Grey* and *The Tenant of Wildfell Hall*. Their brother Branwell, who went from one job as a portrait painter or a tutor to another with little success, died depressed and addicted to gin and opium at the age of thirty-one.

After their sisters' deaths, Partrick Brontë removed Charlotte and Emily from the Clergy Daughters' School. At home Charlotte, Emily, Anne, and Branwell read extensively from the books in their father's well-furnished library, especially the novels of Sir Walter Scott, the poetry of Lord Byron, and *The Arabian Nights*. They began writing stories and poetry themselves, particularly sagas concerning two fictional kingdoms, Angria and Gondal.

From 1831 through 1832, Charlotte was a pupil at the Roe Head School. In 1835, she became a teacher there, and remained until 1838. In 1839, she became a governess, and worked for several families in Yorkshire. With Emily in 1842, Charlotte left England and enrolled in the Pensionat Heger in Brussels, Belgium. In exchange for tuition and board, Charlotte taught English at the school, and Emily taught music. They were called home in October because of the death of their aunt, who had come to look after them and their father after their mother died. Charlotte returned to the school by herself in January 1843. Her second stay was difficult. Charlotte was in love with Professor Heger, and his relation to her was very warm. His wife soon became jealous, and Heger became cold to Charlotte. She returned home after a year.

With her sisters, Emily and Anne, Charlotte began writing in earnest. In 1846, the Brontës, using the pseudonyms Acton, Currer, and Ellis Bell, published a volume of poetry. It was neither a commercial nor a critical success, but the Brontës persisted. Emily wrote *Wuthering Heights;* Anne, *Agnes Grey;* and Charlotte, *Jane Eyre.* The three novels were all published in 1847. All three were commercial and critical successes. But Emily died of tuberculosis in 1848, shortly after her brother Branwell's death, and Anne died of the same disease in 1849. Charlotte nursed each one. While doing so, she nevertheless continued writing. In 1849, *Shirley*, her third novel, but the second to be published, appeared. Her first novel, *The Professor,* was repeatedly rejected when she first submitted it, and was published only after her death.

Brontë, the only surviving member of the family, lived with and took care of her aging father in the Village of Haworth, but, encouraged by her publisher because of the great success of *Jane Eyre,* she made occasional trips to London. She no longer concealed her identity, and in London met and became friendly with the novelist, William Makepeace Thackeray, author of *Vanity Fair;* Elizabeth Gaskell, the novelist and Brontë's first biographer; and the writer and psychologist, G.H. Lewes, who was the life-long companion of the novelist George Eliot.

In 1854, Brontë married her father's curate, Arthur Bell Nicholls. She died nine months later, during pregnancy, either of tuberculosis or, more likely, typhus, contracted from her housekeeper. Brontë was buried in the family vault in The Church of St. Michael and All Angels in West Yorkshire.

The Story Behind the Story

Jane Eyre is a book by a young woman who read books. That is not to say that *Jane Eyre* is not alive with real human passion, indignation, conflict, and frustration, or that actual events in Charlotte Brontë's own life and in the lives of people close to her did not serve to inspire some of the characters and events of the novel. They did.

Charlotte Brontë and her sister Anne both were, like Jane Eyre, governesses. Anne was a governess, in fact, in the same household, the Robinson's, where their brother Branwell was also employed as a tutor. He was dismissed when Mr. Robinson, the head of the household, discovered that Branwell was involved in an amorous liaison with his wife. Their romance, regardless of whether it was hardly realized or full-blown, provides a kernel of the central plot of *Jane Eyre*—the romance between a governess and her master, to the consternation of his wife.

The story of attraction between a younger woman and a married older man was also the story of Jane's relation with Constantin Heger. Heger was the teacher at the Pensionat Heger, in Brussels, Belgium, where Jane and her sister Emily both studied and were employed as instructors. With Heger, Jane shared an intellectual closeness that turned into love, but his wife crushed any possibility of their affection by her opposition to their relationship. Heger withdrew, becoming distant and cold to the pupil whose great gifts he had recognized.

Like Jane, Charlotte also went to a harsh school where severity was practiced in the name of Christianity. And two of her sisters, Elizabeth and Maria, died, like Helen Burns, of tuberculosis contracted there. Like Jane, too, Charlotte attended and taught at a school where pupils were well treated, the Roe Head School. This served as the model for Lowood after the institution had undergone humane reform.

Jane, too, in her small and far from physically beautiful appearance, resembled her creator. And the core of *Jane Eyre*, the story of the mad wife in the attic, also has a model in reality. Near the town of Leeds, in England, a governess married a man employed by the family she served as a governess. After a year of marriage to him, the fact emerged that he was already married. His excuse for committing bigamy was that his wife was mad.

Brontë wove these events into a fiction that incorporates several characteristics of the novel as it had developed until 1847. Primarily, *Jane Eyre* is a Gothic novel. The Gothic novel was a creation of Horace Walpole, who published the prototype of the genre in 1764, *The Castle of Otranto*. Gothic novels are set in castles or houses like castles, such as Thornfield with its battlements. They contain secret staircases and hidden rooms, and there is an air of mystery, secrecy, and threat connected to them. Strange, ominous, even supernatural events seem to occur in them. Such castles and such novels are home to a dark, brooding, mysterious, and potentially dangerous man. The heroine of the gothic novel is always a young woman in distress and threatened by the lord of the Gothic castle. Love, and parted lovers, as well as unlawful love, are also essential elements of the Gothic novels. All these elements, varied although they are, play an important part in *Jane Eyre*.

The theme of the heroine in distress threatened by a duplicitous lover predates the Gothic and is at the heart of the long epistolary novels—novels which are written in the form of letters—like *Pamela* and *Clarissa* by Samuel Richardson, 1689–1761. Another mainstay of the English novel was the presence of uncertain parentage and the discovery of true parentage at the end of the novel, conjoined with the arrival of an unexpected inheritance that confers wealth and status.

In their father's library, as children, the Brontës not only read but they also wrote, and they shared with each other what they wrote. After she returned home from Brussels, Charlotte began, with her sisters, to write in earnest. The Brontës had written poetry and epics since childhood. Then, in 1846, the three sisters chose male pen names to lend authority to their authorial voices, and published a volume of poems by Acton, Currer, and Ellis Bell. Although this enterprise was a dismal failure, each of the sisters continued writing the novel she had undertaken. The next year saw the publication of Anne's *Agnes Grey*, Emily's *Wuthering Heights*, and Charlotte's *Jane Eyre*.

List of Characters

Jane Eyre is the narrator/heroine of the novel. Left as an infant with a cruel aunt and her three spoilt children, Jane grows to be a small, quiet, withdrawn girl, nevertheless intelligent, keen, and possessing a strong sense of duty and justice. She speaks boldly and honestly even when bullied. After eight years at a charity boarding school she becomes the governess at Thornfield for Rochester's ward, Adele.

Edward Rochester is a dark, brooding, introverted man, who finds in Jane companionship, understanding, and love. He secretly keeps his first wife, insane and ferocious, locked in the attic of his house. His marriage to Jane is interrupted by the revelation that he already has a wife. When his mad wife escapes from her confinement and sets fire to his house, he becomes blind and loses his right hand.

Mrs. Reed, Jane's aunt, embodies the figure of the cruel stepmother. She hates Jane, her husband's sister's child. At his death he asked his wife to promise that she care for Jane, but she and her family treat her with disdain and severity.

John Reed, Mrs. Reed's son and Jane's cousin, bullies and beats her in his youth. He grows into a debauched wastrel who finally commits suicide and is the death of his mother.

Georgiana Reed is Mrs. Reed's elder daughter and John's sister. She grows into a beautiful but spoiled, selfish, and lazy young woman.

Eliza Reed, her sister, is her opposite, plain, devout and cold.

Bessie is one of Mrs. Reed's servants, Bessie is the only one in the Reed household who treats Jane with some kindness and tenderness.

Miss Abbot is one of the servants in Mrs. Reed's house.

Robert is Bessie's husband.

Mr. Lloyd is an apothecary who treats Jane after her night confined in the red room as punishment makes her ill. He suggests the idea of going away to school to her.

Mr. Brocklehurst is the founder of the Lowood Institution, the school to which Jane is sent. He is a cruel, hypocritical man who uses Christianity to frighten and coerce children into obedience, with ideas of sudden death and eternal confinement in hell.

Miss Temple is the kindly headmistress of Lowood.

Miss Scatcherd is a teacher at Lowood who is particularly cruel to Helen Burns.

Miss Miller is a teacher at Lowood.

Helen Burns is a pupil at Lowood. She is ill with consumption, and is treated cruelly at school and punished humiliatingly for minor faults. She cultivates a quiet Christian acceptance of her burdens, and when she dies, Jane is with her.

Mary Ann Wilson is a pupil and Jane's friend at Lowood.

Mrs. Fairfax is Rochester's housekeeper.

Celine Varens, a French opera dancer who was Rochester's mistress, appears only in a flashback, when Rochester tells Jane the story of his infatuation with her when he was a young man in Paris.

Adele Varens is her daughter and possibly Rochester's. He does not acknowledge paternity but has assumed the responsibility for her upbringing.

Bertha Mason is the woman Rochester married in Jamaica, West Indies, who turns out to be mad and whom he keeps locked in the attic.

Grace Poole is the servant who occupies the attic room with Bertha Mason as her keeper and guard.

John Mason is Bertha Mason's brother. When he visits her at Thornfield, Rochester's home, she attacks him.

Mr. Woods is the clergyman who conducts Jane and Rochester's interrupted marriage ceremony.

Mr. Briggs is a London solicitor. Warned about Rochester's living wife by John Mason, he interrupts their wedding ceremony. Later, it is Briggs who informs the Rivers family that he is looking for Jane Eyre in order to bestow her uncle's bequest upon her.

Blanche Ingram is a rich and beautiful but haughty and shallow young woman who wishes to marry Rochester.

St. John Rivers is a clergyman who shelters Jane when he finds her starving on his doorstep after she has left Rochester. He is young, handsome, and devout but also cold. He plans on being a missionary in India and proposes to Jane that she marry him and become his assistant in India.

Mary Rivers is his sister and works as a governess.

Diana Rivers is also his sister, and, like Mary, a governess. Both extend their warmth to Jane when she is a stranger among them.

Hannah is their housekeeper. She denies Jane's request for shelter when she comes to their door.

Rosamond Oliver is the beautiful and sweet daughter of a wealthy manufacturer. She is in love with St. John, but he sacrifices his affection for her and cannot think of marrying her because she is not made to be a missionary and accompany him to India.

Mr. Oliver is Rosamond's father. He endows the school that Jane runs after she has left Rochester.

John Eyre is Jane's rich uncle in Maderira who leaves his fortune to her.

Summary and Analysis

Written in the form of an autobiography, the novel *Jane Eyre* traces the growth of its heroine/narrator as she confronts and overcomes adversity and challenges. Set in the villages of the English countryside during the first half of the nineteenth century, *Jane Eyre* is the story of an impoverished, despised, and mistreated orphan who lives until the age of ten at the home of her wealthy, haughty Aunt Reed. At ten she is sent to a miserable charity school and there grows into an earnest, witty, self-disciplined, and practical young woman. She will be strong enough to confront temptation, disappointment, and hardship, as well as bear good fortune with equanimity. She possesses an equal amount of concern for her own welfare and the welfare of others.

In Chapter Five, the overture of *Jane Eyre* is concluded as the ten year old girl is removed from her aunt's home and sent to Lowood Institution, a severe and inhospitable charity school for girls. She remains at Lowood until her eighteenth year, through Chapter Ten, when she leaves to take a position as governess at Thornfield, the residence of Edward Rochester, where she will be tutor to his ward, Adele. From Chapter Eleven through Chapter Twenty-seven, the major part of the book, Charlotte Brontë tells the story of the romance between Jane Eyre and her mysterious and moody master, Edward Rochester.

At the end of Chapter Twenty-seven, Jane flees Thornfield, loving Rochester but unable to marry him, and sets out on her own with but twenty-shillings to start life again. After she arrives at Whitcross, homeless and hungry, chapters Twenty-eight through Thirty-six tell the story of how Jane makes a new life and how the challenges and temptations she encounters further her growth and self-definition. At Chapter Thirty-six, the coda of the novel begins as Jane returns to Thornfield and Edward Rochester.

Divided into these five sections, *Jane Eyre* combines elements of the Gothic novel, the episodic novel, and the novel of childhood and family. Overall it is a *Bildungsroman*, a novel that recounts the intellectual, psychological, and moral development of a character who is shaped by encountering life's challenges and her responses to them. Its central section is a Gothic Romance, set in a dark and eerie mansion, full of secrets and mystery, presided over by a dark lord who is himself marked by secrets and mystery. The surrounding landscape is a picture of wild and perhaps haunted nature. The novel introduces a variety of characters, uninvolved with each other but joined to the plot of the novel by their connection to Jane, like the spokes of a wheel.

The **first four chapters** of *Jane Eyre* establish simultaneously Jane's narrative authority and the strength of her character. The reader is quickly convinced of her reliability as a narrator because of the combination of integrity, strength, and vulnerability she conveys. Her description of the physical world is sharp, and her delineation of the characters of the people around her, generous. Even when she does not like them, they resonate as three dimensional, even if terribly limited, beings. Her presentation of herself is always modest and distanced.

As *Jane Eyre* begins, Jane and her three cousins are coming indoors on a bleak rainy winter day after finding that a walk outside is impossible. While the Reed children are in the drawing room "clustered round" their mother, Jane is banished to "a small breakfast-room adjoining the drawing-room," because she lacked, according to her aunt, "a … sociable and childlike disposition, a[n] … attractive and sprightly manner." But that is not what the reader sees; the reader sees a sweet, unassuming girl quietly coping; she counts on her own self-reliance to get through the rejection and isolation. Jane is an admirable, resilient, and imaginative little girl. She is also shown as neither impertinent nor cowed. Mrs. Reed regards Jane's desire to know what her fault is as violence against authority, but the reader cannot but see it as fair inquiry.

Ensconced in a window seat and half hidden behind the draperies, Jane sits with a book of exotic birds and describes the pictures she looks at and her flights of fancy until her quiet is broken by the intrusion of her Reed cousins, and primarily by John Reed. With swagger he asks her by what right she has taken one of his books. He demands it back from her, and after she hands it to him, he throws it at her. Dodging it, she falls and cuts her head upon the door behind her.

When Jane reproaches him for being a "'wicked and cruel boy' … he ran headlong at me," attacking her and pulling her hair. In frenzy, Jane fights back. When Mrs. Reed and the servants run in, summoned by John's sisters, Jane is called "a fury" who had flown at "Master John, and is dragged to "the red room."

The red room is an unused bedchamber in which her uncle, Mrs. Reed's husband and Jane's dead mother's brother, died nine years earlier. He had loved his unfortunate niece; on his deathbed he made his wife swear to take care of her, but she breached her promise. In the red room Jane is overcome by a fear of ghosts. At evening, frantic, she pounds on the door in terror. Mrs. Reed ignores her supplication and keeps her locked in the room. Jane has "a species of fit: unconsciousness closed the scene."

When she wakes in the morning, back in her own bed, she is ill and being attended by Mr. Lloyd, the apothecary. Bessie, one of Mrs. Reed's servants, and more tender in her treatment of Jane than the rest of the household, is at the foot of her bed. Questioning Jane, Lloyd learns of her unhappiness at Gateshead and when he asks if she would rather go away to school than stay with Mrs. Reed, Jane says yes.

In a conversation between Bessie and another servant she overhears, Jane learns for the first time,

> that my father had been a poor clergyman; that my mother had married him against the wishes of her friends, who considered the match beneath her; that my grandfather Reed was so irritated at her disobedience, he cut her off without a shilling; that after my mother and father had been married a year, the latter caught the typhus fever … that my mother took the infection from him, and both died within a month of each other.

Chapter Four is a bridge, moving Jane from Gateshead to the Lowood Institution where she will remain for eight years, six as a student and two as a teacher. At Lowood, the raw character that Brontë has presented in the first four chapters is refined and becomes the woman Jane is when she leaves the school for Mr. Rochester's house at Thornfield.

Before Jane leaves the Reeds and Gateshead, Mr. Brocklehurst, the clergyman who runs Lowood, visits to interview Jane. Cruel, hypocritical, selfish, and bullying, he is a man who uses Christianity as a club with which to beat or threaten others, especially children. Jane dreads him, and Mrs. Reed gives her more cause by telling Brocklehurst that Jane is a deceitful child. Jane worries that Mrs. Reed's ill-report will accompany her to Lowood, tainting her reputation there.

In her last days at Gateshead Jane finds a lessening of the distress. Mrs. Reed cuts off all contact between herself, her children, and Jane, having been mortified, after Brocklehurst left, when Jane asserted herself to say that she was not deceitful, and that she had suffered from being ill-treated and unloved. In addition, Bessie begins to treat Jane with more kindness than she previously had after Jane's terrible night in the red room, and she confesses to Jane, too, "you are rather put upon, that's certain. My mother said, when she came to see me last week, that she would not like a little one of her own to be in your place." Bessie's mother's observation validates Jane's point of view.

Chapters Five through Ten recount Jane's eight years at Lowood, but concentrate on her first year. "This is not to be a regular autobiography," Jane writes. "I am only bound to invoke Memory where I know her responses will possess some degree of interest." When she first arrives, Lowood is a forbidding place governed by cruelty. The girls live in squalor, and in the bitter cold. They are fed hardly edible meager portions and disciplined by humiliation. The specter of Mr. Brocklehurst looms above the entire institution. He preaches poverty, plainness, and sacrifice while his family live in gaudy luxury. Lowood, nevertheless, is a positive experience for Jane. She proves herself, despite Brocklehurst's public denunciation of her as a liar, to be honest, diligent, capable, and friendly. Her closest friend is Helen Burns, who is dying, although Jane does not know it, of consumption. Despite her ill-health and her excellence as a student, Helen Burns is relentlessly harassed by her teachers. Helen responds to the burdens of humiliation and punishment with modest acquiescence and calmness of spirit, which serves to instruct Jane in the power of an indomitable inner strength. Jane also is self-reliant, although she never assumes the self-effacing disposition and martyrdom that define Helen Burns.

The terrible conditions at Lowood breed an epidemic of typhoid fever, but Jane is not infected. The death of a number of the girls at the school, however, brings attention to the squalid conditions. Consequently, Brocklehurst's power and authority are reduced, a board of directors is established, and through her remaining tenure, Lowood is a far more humane place than it had been when Jane entered. When she leaves, it is because the Headmistress, Miss Temple, who has always been kind to Jane, is leaving to be married. Without Miss Temple, Jane feels no connection to the school.

Unsure what to do, Jane decides to become a governess. With the dispatch that has become characteristic of her and which she will exercise throughout the rest of her narrative, Jane responds to a newspaper advertisement for a governess. When she is offered a position in the distant village of Millcote, she leaves Lowood, venturing as a stranger into a world she will make her own, a world readers will recognize as belonging to the genre of the Gothic novel.

Before Jane leaves Lowood, however, Brontë begins to weave the strands of the novel together. Hearing that Jane is about to set off for a distant part of England, Bessie, Mrs. Reed's housekeeper visits her, and with her brings news of the Reed family, particularly that John Reed has grown into a dissipated wastrel who is living a debauched life in London, and depleting his mother's fortune and, by his conduct, wrecking her health.

Jane arrives at Thornfield Hall believing that Mrs. Fairfax, who placed the advertisement, is her employer and the mother of her pupil. But Mrs. Fairfax is the housekeeper. The child

Adele Varens is the "ward" of Thornfield's master, Edward Rochester, who spends long periods of time away from Thornfield. Inside Thornfield Hall, a vast and gloomy three-storey mansion with battlements round the top, "a very chill and vault-like air pervaded the stairs and gallery, suggesting cheerless ideas of space and solitude." There lurks within, too, the presentiment of something disquieting, and it is made tangible when Mrs. Fairfax takes Jane on a tour of the mansion and upon descending from the roof through the attic Jane hears "a curious laugh ... mirthless ... at first ... very low," but which became "a clamorous peal that seemed to wake an echo in every lonely chamber." Mrs. Fairfax suggests that it is one of the servants, Grace Poole. But Jane is left with a lingering doubt, obliquely expressed in her description of "the long passage ... separating the front and back rooms of the third storey: narrow, low, and dim, with only one little window at the far end, and looking, with its two rows of small black doors all shut, like a corridor in some Bluebeard's castle." Her allusion to Bluebeard conjures the image of the nobleman who wed and murdered a series of wives and immured their remains in his castle. The foreboding architecture and the disquieting laugh and the thought of Bluebeard, however, are offset by the cheerful quality of Jane's own chamber, which is "a bright little place" where "the sun shone in between the gay blue chintz window curtains, showing papered walls and a carpeted floor, so unlike the bare planks and stained plaster of Lowood."

Her first three months at Thornfield pass quietly. Mrs. Fairfax is the kindly creature she seemed to be; Adele, is tractable and affectionate. But Jane "desired more of practical experience than I possessed; more of intercourse with my kind, of acquaintance with variety of character, than was here within my reach." Her wish is fulfilled when she meets Rochester under circumstances that foreshadow the stormy and obscure course their romance will follow. A cold January afternoon, Jane has given Adele a holiday from school work and has set out on a walk to Hay to post a letter for Mrs. Fairfax. Her path is a deserted one. The ground is hard and frozen. The sun is low. The church bell tolls. Then everything is still.

No cattle graze in the fields. It is a brooding and isolated landscape, unawakened from winter sleep. Jane rests by the ice-coated roadside on a stile, near a frozen brook, protected from the cold by her cloak, her hands in her muff. From "far away," but clearly, she hears the clattering of horse hooves on the hard earth. She imagines the horse to be some phantom heath monster until the horse, its rider, and his dog running alongside, pass by her. Immediately after, she hears the noise of a fall and the cry of the rider's curse. The dog runs to her as if seeking her help. She approaches the fallen man with an offer of aid. With Jane's help, despite a sprained ankle, Rochester manages to remount his horse and proceeds to Thornfield as Jane, who as yet does not know who he is, continues on to Hay.

Although Jane does not know who the man she has helped is, she intuits quite a bit about him and about herself from their encounter. Rochester, "enveloped in a riding cloak, fur collared and steel clasped," suggests a hidden man muffled up in mystery. "Of middle height and considerable breadth of chest," he is powerful and yet in some unaccountable way, dwarfed, not grown to his full size. His face is "a dark face, with stern features and a heavy brow; his eyes and gathered eyebrows looked ireful and thwarted ... he was past youth, but had not reached middle-age; perhaps he might be thirty-five." Jane "felt no fear of him, and but little shyness." She knows, however, that "[h]ad he been a handsome, heroic-looking young gentleman, I should not have dared to stand thus questioning him against his will, and offering my services unasked," because "I should have known instinctively that [he] neither had nor could have sympathy with anything in me." Moreover, "if even this stranger had smiled and been good-humored to me when I addressed him; if he had put off my offer of assistance gaily and with thanks, I should have gone on my way and not felt any vocation to renew inquiries: but the frown, the roughness of the traveler, set me at my ease." She sees him as a man, not an ideal. It is her particular intelligence to see in his roughness a sign of his weakness. What lingers of the scene for Jane is that she had performed a necessary even if rather trivial service and that Rochester's face was "dark, strong, and stern." His return transforms Thornfield the very next morning from a dull house into a place bustling with excitement. "It echoed every hour or two to a knock at the door, or a clang of the bell; steps ... often traversed the hall, and new voices spoke in different keys below; a rill from the outer world was flowing through it."

The evening of his first day at Thornfield, Rochester summons Jane to meet him in the library. He reviews her past history and qualifications, listens to her play the piano and looks at her drawings. Despite the formality of their relationship, the reader can sense the undercurrent of personal feelings and the tension of two strong but contrasting personalities. Although Jane is a small woman and delicate and Rochester broad and gruff, her power and self-control exceed his. She sees him as a species of brute manhood; he regards her as an elf or fairy. By the end of their meeting, she thinks he is quite peculiar and the reader can easily share her view. He seems supercilious, and his moods are changeful. When Jane remarks on the peculiarity of his character to Mrs. Faifax, the housekeeper offers that "if he has peculiarities of temper, allowance should be made ... [p]artly because it is his nature ... and partly because he has painful thoughts ... to harass him, and make his spirits unequal."

Rochester has "[f]amily troubles" Mrs. Fairfax says. Her account of them, however, is vague and incomplete. He had an older brother, Rowland, who died some nine years ago, and it was then, he came into his property, which otherwise would have been his brother's, not his. Before that, when his fortune was not secure, "Old Mr. Rochester and Mr. Rowland combined to bring Mr. Edward into what he considered a painful position, for the sake of making his fortune: what the precise nature of that position was I never clearly knew, but his spirit could not brook what he had to suffer in it." That is all the reader will learn for a while. Just as Thornfield has a mystery buried within it, so its master has a mystery buried inside him.

As Jane and Rochester begin to deepen their acquaintance, he becomes increasingly aware of a power in her to draw him out, to listen to him with serious interest but never flattering him or repressing the expression of her own opinions. He begins to talk about himself and his faults, first in generalities, simply confessing that he has faults, as though wishing for absolution from her. The effect of his conversation, mostly, however, is to bewilder her.

In **Chapter Fifteen**, Rochester becomes more specific, filling in the details of his past. He reveals to Jane the story of his youthful folly in Paris and how Adele became his ward. As a young man, he had a mistress, the French "opera dancer," Celine Varens, Adele's mother. Possibly he is Adele's father, although he is not sure. Nevertheless, when Celine abandoned the child he took responsibility for her, although without acknowledging paternity. His love affair with Celine is the story of a gold-digging beauty who charmed, seduced, and betrayed him. As important a piece of Rochester's history as this story is, the event that follows his telling of it, shows that what happened in Paris is less significant than something else in his past that yet remains a mystery.

In her bed-chamber just after the clock has struck two, Jane hears footsteps outside the door. Startled, she thinks, at first, it must be Pilot, Rochester's dog, padding about, but she hears the same demonical laugh she heard when Mrs. Fairfax took her through the attic to show her the surrounding countryside from Thornfield's battlements. Quietly opening the door to her room, Jane sees an indistinct figure at the end of the hall and smoke escaping from under the door to Rochester's bed-chamber. Inside his room, Jane finds the bed curtains aflame and her master asleep. Taking the pitcher from his washstand she douses the fire with water, rushes to her own room for more water and drenches the bed, finally waking its sleeper, who remains quite unfazed, despite the occurrence. "In the name of all the elves in Christendom, is that Jane Eyre?" are his first words. "What have you done with me witch, sorceress.... Have you plotted to drown me?" he teases her.

He does not, however, lack control of the situation. He forbids Jane to fetch a servant, instructs her to wait for him, and soon returns saying, "it is just as I thought." When she responds, "How, sir?" he makes no reply but only questions her with regard to what she saw. And when she indicates that she thinks Grace Poole is the source of the mischief, he says, "Just so. Grace Poole—you have guessed it," which the reader suspects and will learn definitively in the course of the story, is a deliberate evasion.

In the morning Jane hears the servants cleaning Rochester's bed-chamber talking among themselves and saying how fortunate their master was and how unwise it is to fall asleep with a lighted candle beside the bed. When she sees Grace Poole herself sitting by Rochester's bedside sewing curtains for the bed to replace the damaged ones, she is perplexed by the puzzle, but unsettled, too, by fear of Grace Poole.

The intimacy, danger, and mystery of the middle-of-the-night fire brings Jane and Rochester closer. His ardor for her keeps escaping in bitten off sentences and small gestures: his reluctance to let her part from him, after the fire, for example. She feels a similar excitement about him, but is a mistress of containing emotion. This mutual excitement makes it all the more disheartening when she does not see Rochester the next day. Mrs. Fairfax informs her that he has left Thornfield to visit a neighboring mansion where guests are gathering for a long visit and that among those guests will be a certain Miss Ingram, known for her beauty, her wealth, and her interest in Rochester. Rather than surrendering to disappointment, however, Jane uses the situation, characteristically, to "arraign" herself "at my own bar," and to "pronounce judgment" against herself, stipulating "that a greater fool than Jane Eyre had never breathed the breath of life" to think that she could be "a favorite with Mr. Rochester," "gifted with the power of pleasing him," or "of importance to him in any way." The sentence that she then imposes on herself is to "draw in chalk your own picture ... without softening one defect" and "write under it, 'Portrait of a Governess, disconnected, poor, and plain.' Afterwards, take a piece of smooth ivory" and "paint ... Blanche Ingram," whom Mrs. Fairfax has described to her. Under this portrait, she instructs herself to write "Blanche, an accomplished lady of rank." She concludes her discipline of self-mortification by instructing herself:

Whenever, in future, you should chance to fancy Mr. Rochester thinks well of you, take out these two pictures and compare them: say, 'Mr. Rochester might probably win that noble lady's love, if he chose to strive for it; is it likely he would waste a serious thought on this indigent and insignificant plebeian?'

After an absence from Thornfield of more than two weeks, Rochester forwards a letter to Mrs. Fairfax informing her that he will be returning in three days with a number of "fine people," guests, moving from their merrymaking at the neighboring estate to his. The household is turned upside down as cleaning, cooking, and anticipation replace the staid routine. In the course of helping with the cooking and reordering of Thornfield, Jane overhears several of the servants talking about Grace Poole, her difficult job, and the high wages Rochester pays her, but when they notice Jane is nearby, they break off their conversation with final whispers about how much Jane does or does not know.

The arrival of Rochester and his guests, the bustle of the servants, and the excitement of continuous merrymaking divert Jane and the reader from further thought of hidden things. Jane's chief occupation is to keep Adele's excitement under control and to chasten her own jealous longing to share in the pleasures of a world from which she is excluded. In **Chapters Seventeen and Eighteen**, Brontë presents a picture of that world, its people, their style, attitudes, and amusements. At the center of the picture, and at the center of Jane's concern, is Blanche Ingram, the haughty beauty it appears that Rochester will marry. Jane surveys everything as a member of the company, at Rochester's insistence, obedient but reluctant, seated, as is befitting a governess, in a recess of the room.

The report Jane makes of Rochester's guests as she observes them from her corner shows them to be haughty and shallow even as they glitter fashionably with wealth. Miss Ingram, there with her mother and two sisters, is at the center of the party, directing conversation and entertainment. Aware and resentful of Jane's presence—it violates her class privilege of not having to associate with people who are her social inferiors—she leads a conversation disparaging governesses. Its effect on the reader is, of course, to elevate Jane higher in esteem and to show Miss Ingram as entirely antipathetic and undesirable, despite her stature, clothing, and beauty.

To amuse themselves, the guests play a game of charades. One team of guests performs a short skit and the other team attempts to guess the word which may characterize the skit. Blanche stars in two skits. In the first, dressed in white, Blanche kneels beside Rochester before an altar. In the second Blanche portrays the biblical Rebecca at the well when the messenger from Abraham comes to claim her as his son Isaac's wife. The words each skit suggests are "bride" and "well," which in combination form "Bridewell," the name of a prison in London. Referring to a famous British institution, the word is innocent enough in the context of a game, but in the context of the unfolding plot of *Jane Eyre*, it is sinister, suggesting a bride locked up. But it cannot have that resonance for Jane who is, as are the readers, unaware of the real secret of Thornfield. For Jane the scenes simply reinforce her conviction that Rochester is heading towards marriage with Blanche Ingram.

One morning, while his guests are still present, Rochester is apparently summoned away on business. Late in the afternoon, a new, unexpected, and unknown guest, John Mason, claiming to be an old friend of Rochester, arrives. He says he has known him in Kingston, Jamaica, in the West Indies. He joins the other guests in the library, but conversation is soon interrupted when a footman enters the drawing room and announces that a gypsy woman is in the kitchen and that she refuses to leave until after she sees all the young women and tells their fortunes. One of the guests, a magistrate, orders that she be set in the stocks, but this is countermanded by the young people, especially by the haughty Miss Ingram, who are eager to hear their fortunes told. When Blanche Ingram returns to the drawing room after her interview with the gypsy, however, "her face grew momently darker, more dissatisfied, and more sourly expressive of disappointment. She had obviously not heard anything to her advantage." The other young ladies return in better cheer, astonished by how much the gypsy knew about them. As the guests talk of the gypsy, a footman whispers to Jane that the gypsy "declares that there is another young single lady in the room who has not been to her yet, and she swears she will not go till she has seen all."

During her conversation with the gypsy, Jane maintains the same moral equilibrium that she displays in every situation. The gypsy elicits to her own satisfaction, nevertheless, that Jane cares for Rochester. As if to encourage Jane's hope, she tells her that the bond Jane seems to observe between Rochester and Blanche Ingram is not a strong one and that she (the gypsy), in her session with Blanche, told her that Rochester's fortune is not as large as it appears to be. (That, the reader can surmise, was the cause of Blanche Ingram's pique upon returning from her meeting with the gypsy.) Describing Jane's character, the gypsy seems to be reading the obstacles to Rochester's love for her. Jane "can live alone, if self-respect, and circumstances require me so to do." She will "not sell my soul to buy bliss." She has "an inward treasure … which can keep me alive if all extraneous delights should be withheld, or offered only at a price I cannot afford to give." In short, the gypsy says of Jane that she will not be dominated by passion but by her conscience, that her sense of right will triumph over the longings of her heart. By the end of her speech the gypsy has metamorphosed into Rochester, and her words, although cryptic when they are uttered now, will become clear as further events unfold. "I have formed my plans," Rochester says, "and in them I have attended to the claims of conscience…. I know how soon youth would fade and bloom perish, if, in the cup of bliss offered, but one dreg of shame, or one flavor of remorse were detected; and I do not want sacrifice." I want, Rochester says, shedding his disguise, "to earn gratitude, not to wring tears of blood." In order to do so, he must keep concealed something he is still concealing.

But what he must conceal is about to reveal itself. After he has uncovered himself, in order to keep Jane with him a little longer, Rochester asks Jane what his guests say about him in his absence. She mentions that a visitor named Mason has arrived. Her news is a blow that staggers him. It elicits from him cryptic questions which suggest awful mystery. "If all these people came in a body and spat at me, what would you do, Jane?" She answers, "Turn them out of the room, sir, if I could." And when he asks her if she "could dare censure for my sake?" she answers, "I could dare it for the sake of any friend who deserved my adherence; as you, I am sure, do."

Cheered by her response, he tells her to go into the drawing room and whisper to Mason that he has returned home and wishes to see him in the library. Because Jane is not present at their colloquy, neither she nor the reader, consequently, knows what went on between them, but as she is going to sleep, Jane hears Rochester cheerfully show Mason his room, and eased at heart, she sleeps. Her sleep is interrupted, however, at the beginning of **Chapter Twenty** "by a savage, a sharp, a shrilly sound that ran from end to end of Thornfield Hall!" The cry was followed by the sounds of struggle in the chamber directly above Jane's and then by a voice calling Rochester for help. Alarmed by the commotion, Rochester's guests rush out of their rooms but he urges them to return, explaining a servant had a nightmare. When the gallery is cleared Rochester knocks on Jane's door and tells her to get dressed, which she has already done in anticipation of being needed, and come help him.

Rochester leads her to a room in the attic. There she finds John Mason, injured and bleeding, ranting about how "she" bit him. Rochester reproaches him for not having heeded his warning. Without being able to see what it is, Jane hears what sounds like the cries of a savage animal coming from an inner, locked room. She assumes it is Grace Poole in a state of frenzy who has attacked Mason. Rochester shows Jane how to sponge Mason's bleeding wound and goes himself to fetch the surgeon, instructing both of them not to speak to each other while he is gone. Any speech, he warns, would provoke agitation in the wounded man and cause his injury to worsen. That, of course, is a ruse. Rochester is guarding a secret.

After the surgeon has attended to Mason's wound, and Rochester has given him a strengthening cordial, as the dawn is unfolding, they put Mason in a carriage to take him away from

Thornfield. He and Rochester exchange cryptic words about taking good care of "her." Jane and Rochester are left sitting in the garden. She is more puzzled than ever about what hold Grace Poole can have on Rochester that he continues to shelter her despite how dangerous she can be. His reply that he can handle Grace Poole provides no real answer, but Jane is the model of submissive love, accepting Rochester as he is because she believes in his fundamental goodness.

"You are my little friend, are you not?" he asks her. She replies, "I like to serve you, sir, and to obey you in all that is right." "Precisely," he replies. "I see you do. I see genuine contentment ... when you are helping me and pleasing me—working for me, and with me, in, 'ALL THAT IS RIGHT:' for if I bid you do what you thought wrong ... [m]y friend would then turn to me, quiet and pale, and would say, 'No, sir; that is impossible: I cannot do it, because it is wrong;' and would become immutable as a fixed star." This wry characterization shows that Rochester is obviously nervous. He is afraid he is on the wrong side of what is right and consequently that his ability to possess her is not assured. In self-defense he puts the following case before her:

> Suppose you were no longer a girl well reared and disciplined, but a wild boy indulged from childhood upwards ... in a remote foreign land; conceive that you there commit a capital error ... one whose consequences must follow you through life and taint all your existence.... I don't say a CRIME; I am not speaking of shedding of blood or any other guilty act ... my word is ERROR. The results of what you have done become in time to you utterly insupportable; you take measures to obtain relief: unusual measures, but neither unlawful nor culpable. Still you are miserable; for hope has quitted you.... you wander here and there, seeking rest in exile: happiness in pleasure.... Heart-weary and soul-withered, you come home after years of voluntary banishment: you make a new acquaintance ... you find in this stranger much of the good and bright qualities which you have

sought for twenty years, and never before encountered; and they are all fresh, healthy, without soil and without taint.... [Y]ou feel better days come back—higher wishes, purer feelings; you desire to recommence your life, and to spend what remains to you of days in a way more worthy of an immortal being. To attain this end, are you justified in overleaping an obstacle of custom—a mere conventional impediment which neither your conscience sanctifies nor your judgment approves?

He is telling her his story and implicitly begging her for something, but his speech is abstract. He gives her nothing by which she can actually see or judge him. Jane remains quiet, unable to respond to a veiled, theoretical question. Rochester repeats his question more insistently, but still vaguely: "'Is the wandering and sinful, but now rest-seeking and repentant, man justified in daring the world's opinion, in order to attach to him for ever this gentle, gracious, genial stranger, thereby securing his own peace of mind and regeneration of life?'" His meaning is plain. He is confessing without saying what he is confessing as a way of proposing marriage to Jane, but she continues to hear him as if he were speaking only of spiritual salvation and not of earthly happiness. "A wanderer's repose or a sinner's reformation should never depend on a fellow-creature," she says. Pushed to the limits of desire, he is on the verge of saying to her that he has found "the instrument" of his redemption in her, but retreats. Instead he becomes cavalier, switches the direction of his speech and talks cynically about how fine an instrument of reformation Miss Ingram will be.

At this knotty place in the gothic plot, Brontë shifts, in **Chapter Twenty-one**, away from the story of Rochester and returns to the story of Jane's family. The day after the commotion and Rochester's ardent but unilluminating revelations, Bessie's husband Robert arrives at Thornfield with news that Mrs. Reed is seriously ill, devastated by John Reed's death. The boy, who bullied and tormented Jane, who grew into a sordid and depraved young man, who drained his mother's wealth, finally committed suicide. In her delirium,

Mrs. Reed has been calling for Jane. Rochester gives Jane permission to leave but insists that she return, and in their conversation reveals again his need for her, and she reveals, again, her ability to stay calm despite her love for him.

Jane's stay at Gateshead and her meeting with her dying Aunt Reed and her two cousins, Eliza and Georgiana, seems to resolve the story of her parentage, her early fate and the Gateshead episode. On her deathbed, Mrs. Reed tells Jane that she had always hated her, that she was jealous of the affection her husband had for his sister, Jane's mother, and then for Jane, after her mother died. Mrs. Reed resented treating Jane, whose parents were poor, as the equal of her children. And she had contempt for Jane because she was not a robust child. But to make this confession was not the reason she called for Jane. Weighing upon her is the fact that she has "twice done you a wrong," she tells Jane. The first wrong, readers are aware of. She broke the promise made to her dying husband, Jane's uncle, to bring her up as her own child. The second wrong she is more reluctant to confess and only does with great difficulty. There had been a letter Mrs. Reed had received three years earlier, while Jane was at Lowood, from a man in Madeira, John Eyre, informing her that he was Jane's uncle. He wrote to ask for Jane's address since "[p]rovidence has blessed my endeavors to secure a competency; and as I am unmarried and childless, I wish to adopt her during my life, and bequeath her at my death whatever I may have to leave." Guided by her bitter resentment of Jane and by a wish to take revenge upon her, Mrs. Reed wrote back that she "was sorry for his disappointment, but Jane Eyre was dead: she had died of typhus fever at Lowood."

Jane hears this confession with the earnest goodness characteristic of her and forgives her aunt and offers her her love. Her aunt, however, did not make the confession in order to be reconciled with her niece, but in the hope of relieving herself of a burden of guilt. In her dying moments she will not even accept a kiss from Jane and insists to the end that Jane has "a very bad disposition." The actual nature of Jane's disposition is shown during her aunt's illness. Mrs. Reed's daughters neglect her and simply wait for her death. Jane is the only one to attend her. After her aunt's death, again, Jane's real goodness is shown by the way she cares for Mrs. Reed's daughters, her two haughty, unfriendly, and condescending cousins, the vain and lazy Georgiana and the overly religious and cold Eliza, before she returns to Thornfield.

As she is returning to Thornfield, despite her sense that because of Rochester's expected marriage to Blanche Ingram, she will not be living there much longer, she looks forward eagerly to seeing him. The situation that greets her on her return, however, does not suggest that she is about to be separated from either the house or its master. Rochester is the first to greet her after she spies him sitting on a stile along her path. He welcomes her home warmly, as if Thornfield were her home. The rest of the household, too, greet her with gladness enhancing her sense of belonging there.

Jane is puzzled, however, by the calmness of Thornfield; it is not like a house in which wedding preparations are being made. Rochester does not even ride the twenty miles it would take to visit Blanche Ingram, his apparent fiancée. One midsummer afternoon, as she walks in the orchard, Jane meets Rochester there and they discuss the future. Rochester seems aloof as he speaks about his impending marriage, his bride to be, and how he will help Jane to find another position. Jane absorbs the facts that she will have to leave Thornfield, and that she and Rochester will never see each other again, and then she breaks down. "I grieve to leave Thornfield," she cries. She asserts,

> I love Thornfield…. I have lived in it a full and delightful life…. I have talked, face to face, with what I reverence, with what I delight in,—with an original, a vigorous, an expanded mind. I have known you, Mr. Rochester; and it strikes me with terror and anguish to feel I absolutely must be torn from you for ever. I see the necessity of departure; and it is like looking on the necessity of death.

As if he had not said anything about getting married or helping to secure her a job in Ireland, Rochester asks, "Where do you see the necessity?" Once he has determined that she does love him, and once he has gotten Jane to show her innermost feelings freely, he abandons his charade and persuades her that he is in earnest when he asks her to marry him. She accepts him joyously. While they talk of love in their edenic garden, the weather changes from fair to stormy, and during the night following their rendezvous, "the great horse-chestnut at the bottom of the orchard [is] struck by lightning … and half of it split away."

Ominous as that is, it has no symbolic meaning for Jane, nor does she notice anything distressing when in the course of a conversation she asks Rochester, to "have the goodness to gratify my curiosity, which is much piqued on one point," and he "looked disturbed" and responded, "Curiosity is a dangerous petition." Unaware of the depth of his response, she teases him, asking, "You will not exclude me from your confidence if you admit me to your heart?" He equivocates: "You are welcome to all my confidence that is worth having, Jane; but for God's sake, don't desire a useless burden! Don't long for poison…. Encroach, presume, and the game is up." Something fatal is being suggested, but she is so full of love for him that she cannot sense that it is. His relief is palpable when her question turns out to be only "Why did you take such pains to make me believe you wished to marry Miss Ingram?"

Rather than the shadows around Rochester, what is occupying Jane's attention is her struggle to maintain her independence as a person even as she gives herself to him. She assures him she is not interested in being bought and kept by means of silks and jewels and treated as a mistress as Cecile Varens was. Warned by Mrs. Fairfax, she keeps him chastely at a distance during the weeks leading up to their wedding. But the mystery surrounding Thornfield and Rochester will not be still. A few nights before their wedding, while Rochester is away on business, Jane is visited by several ominous dreams. The last seems more than a dream. At first she thinks it is an apparition. There is the figure of a woman with a candle going through Jane's wedding things. Finally she takes the veil Jane will wear and rips it, throws it to the floor and tramples upon it. Then she disappears. The torn veil on the floor in the morning convinces Jane that an actual person had been in her room, not a phantom, although in its savagery, it was like no one she has ever seen. When Jane relates the scene to Rochester the next day, he persuades her that it was Mrs. Poole who was in the room behaving in her usually strange way and that feverishly, Jane altered the woman's appearance. Once again Jane allows herself to be placated. She thinks no more about the incident, or wonders why such a one as Grace Poole is tolerated in the house or what can be her hold on Rochester.

The wedding, in **Chapter Twenty-six** brings to a climax the gothic romance when the marriage ceremony is interrupted by a Mr. Briggs, a solicitor, who asserts that Rochester is already married and produces John Mason, who testifies that Rochester married his sister, Bertha Mason, fifteen years earlier in Spanish Town, Jamaica. Rochester admits the truth of the claim and the wedding is cancelled. Instead, Rochester performs a different ceremony. He takes Briggs, Mason, Woods, the clergyman who would have performed the wedding, and Jane up to the attic where Bertha Mason is confined and kept in the care of Grace Poole and shows her to them in her frantic condition. After that, Briggs explains how he knew of the wedding.

Learning of John Eyre from Mrs. Reed, Jane had written to him in Funchal, on the island of Madeira, off the coast of Portugal, and in the course of the letter told him of her impending marriage to Rochester. By coincidence, John Mason was stopping in Madeira on his way back to Jamaica from England and met John Eyre. Eyre told him of his niece's marriage. Distressed, Mason told John Eyre that the man, Rochester, to whom he referred, was married to his sister. Unable to travel himself, John Eyre entreated Mason to return to London, go to Briggs, his solicitor, and save his niece from a compromising marriage.

Jane responds to the exposure of Rochester's secret as she always responds to crises. After reproaching herself for her failure to see things more clearly before the catastrophe arrived, she sets herself to thinking and decides she must leave Rochester and Thornfield. Rochester implores her to stay. He defends his deception by his love. He swears he intended no dishonor should come to her. She forgives him and she admits that she still loves him. She confesses that it would grieve her to leave him. Nevertheless, she insists, she must leave him rather than live with him, even if it is only in mistaken appearance, as his mistress. The next morning before anyone is up, Jane leaves Thornfield on tiptoe with nothing but twenty shillings and a small packet of food she has managed to assemble and sets out by coach to a district far from Rochester.

The coach sets her down at Whitcross, which is nothing more than a road sign in the middle of a moor. Jane walks to the nearest village, tired, cold, and having left her small parcel of food in the coach, hungry. She looks for work unsuccessfully, sleeps outside on the heath for two nights, and is reduced to begging. Wandering and hopeless on the third evening, Jane approaches a cottage whose light she saw from the distance. Before knocking to beg for food and a place to sleep, she peers in at a low window and sees two women "young, graceful women—ladies in every point" dressed in mourning—with their housekeeper, by the fire, studying German together. Through the window Jane sees family warmth and congeniality even in the face of death: their father's. Here is everything from which Jane is excluded. When she goes to the door, Hannah, the housekeeper, will not let her enter or speak to either of the young women. She offers her a piece of bread and a penny, but refuses to let her stay on the property to sleep even in one of the out buildings. She closes the door and leaves Jane on the doorstep in the cold and wet.

"I cannot but die" and await God's "will in silence," Jane says to herself but the voice of a man standing behind her says, "All men must die, but all are not condemned to meet a lingering and premature doom, such as yours would be if you perished here of want." It is St. John Rivers speaking. He is the brother of the two young women Jane has watched sitting by the fireside. Seated soon in her dripping garments before that same fireside, Jane appears pale, wasted, and famished. The two sisters and their brother slowly feed her bread and milk, but when they ask her who she is, she has not the strength to speak. Rather than being seen as any kind of threat, Jane is now cared for with tenderness and put to sleep in a warm bed.

The sisters and their brother care for Jane and develop a strong affection for her. They recognize that she is not a beggar but a young woman well-educated and determined to be self-reliant. Until her strength is restored, Jane lives with Diana, Mary, and St. John. When she is strong again, St. John obtains a position for her as a teacher of poor girls in a village schoolhouse he has persuaded the wealthy Mr. Oliver, a local manufacturer, to establish. There is a cottage close by for her to live in. Jane proves to be an inspiring teacher and gains the affection of her students.

While his sisters are warm-hearted in their affection, St. John, a pillar of virtue and a practitioner of Christian charity, is a cold idealist. He is also, unlike Rochester, exquisitely handsome. He has no secret past or psychic dark places. Passion does not motivate his actions or desires, but a rigid determination to live the life of a Christian and to spread Christian doctrine and offer Christian comfort and aid to the impoverished as a missionary in India. Although he finds Mr. Oliver's beautiful daughter Rosamond alluring, he coldly overcomes the weakness of attraction to earthly delights, to a rose of the world, as the name Rosamond suggests. Her temperament does not lend itself to the sacrificing life of service to which he has dedicated himself. Like Rochester, he discovers in Jane something he senses he needs which can complete him, and he encourages her to dedicate herself to the work he wishes to undertake and, consequently, to him. He asks her to marry him and accompany him as a missionary to India. Seeking purpose for her life and believing in his virtue and the virtue of his mission, Jane is willing to join him as his assistant, but she is unable to accept his offer of marriage. He is not moved by love for her, nor is he sensitive to her as an individual. He wants to enlist her as soldier-wife in a great missionary crusade. His love is cold and all-consuming. Rochester's need for her was great. But it was not overwhelming and destructive as Jane feels St. John's is. Rochester, unlike St. John, presented himself as an actual human being, a man imperfect and knotty and, wanting her for herself. Consequently, he was as a man to whom she could offer her love. St. John wishes to vanquish the man in himself and thus must ignore the woman's heart in Jane.

Although she refuses to marry St. John, Jane does not refuse to accompany him to India as his curate, as if she were his sister. In fact, it turns out she is his cousin. When asked her name the night she was given shelter, Jane said she was Jane Elliott, and admitted that it was a false name when St. John doubted it. Nevertheless, her privacy was respected. St. John discovers her true identity when he sees her real name, Jane Eyre, scribbled on a piece of paper Jane had used to mix colors for her drawings. His discovery of her identity allows him to reveal more of her identity than she knows. They are cousins and her uncle has left his fortune to her. It is the same uncle who had disappointed the Rivers' expectations a week or so earlier when they learned he had not left his fortune to them but to Jane Eyre, whom St. John and his sisters did not know was Jane Elliott's true identity. It is the same uncle to whom Mrs. Reed had written three years earlier that Jane had died, and who had sent John Mason to prevent Jane's marriage to Rochester. When she learns that she has inherited twenty thousand pounds and that her cousins have gotten nothing, she insists on sharing it, dividing the inheritance into four equal parts.

With Rochester, Jane had to exercise self-control over her passion. With St. John, she has to exercise self-control over her tendency to surrender to duty. It may be an even more difficult struggle, especially because, rather than speaking for himself, St. John speaks to Jane's higher duties to God and to herself as if he were God's very voice. But Jane has a strong sense of herself and is clear-minded. She asserts against St. John that

> God did not give me my life to throw away; and to do as you wish me would ... be almost equivalent to committing suicide.... [B]efore I definitively resolve on quitting England, I will know for certain whether I cannot be of greater use by remaining in it than by leaving it.... I can go nowhere till by some means that doubt is removed.

St. John responds,

> I know where your heart turns and to what it clings. The
> interest you cherish is lawless and unconsecrated. Long
> since you ought to have crushed it: now you should blush
> to allude to it. You think of Mr. Rochester?

"It was true," Jane admits. "I confessed it by silence."

St. John is relentless. He nearly persuades Jane to
capitulate: "I could decide if I were but certain," I answered:
"were I but convinced that it is God's will I should marry you,
I could vow to marry you here and now—come afterwards
what would!" "My prayers are heard!" St. John responds,
prematurely, for just as she is wavering, Jane is overwhelmed.
She hears a voice, Rochester's, calling, "Jane! Jane! Jane!"—
nothing more. She cries, "I am coming! Wait for me! Oh, I
will come!" She writes that, "I broke from St. John, who had
followed, and would have detained me. It was MY time to
assume ascendancy. MY powers were in play and in force. I
told him to forbear question or remark; I desired him to leave
me: I must and would be alone."

When Jane returns to Thornfield, eager with anticipation,
she finds that the house was "a blackened ruin," with "shattered
walls" and a "devastated interior." She goes back to the inn
nearby to learn what she can. The first part of what the
innkeeper tells her is in large part her own story. After her
departure, the innkeeper tells her, Rochester remained at
Thornfield, sought her unsuccessfully, grew "savage" and
dismissed his servants, although pensioning them handsomely.
Two months after Jane's departure, Bertha Mason got out
of her attic jail one night when Grace Poole had taken too
much gin, and started a fire in what had been Jane's bed. The
fire spread. Bertha climbed onto the roof and threw herself
to the ground from the battlements of the flaming building.
Rochester was injured in the fire, his right hand crushed and
his eyes blinded. The innkeeper finishes his tale by informing
Jane that Rochester has moved to his other house, Ferndean,
and prepares the chaise to take her there.

As she approaches Ferndean, Jane sees Rochester step out onto the porch and stretch out his hand as if he were checking for rain. It is the gesture of a blind man feeling his way. She does not approach him. Once he is inside, she goes to the door. The servants, who knew her at Thornfield, recognize and welcome her, and when Mary must take candles and a glass of water in to Rochester, Jane takes her place and, in that way, serving him from the first moment, makes herself known to him.

Their scene is the happy ending to the novel. Rochester cannot believe that Jane is real and not a phantom or an elf, and she teases him out of the black depth of his own self-involvement as she always has. Rochester, moreover, cannot believe when Jane offers to stay with him and care for him that she means to do it as his wife. As in the past, she could not believe that he could wish to marry her, now he fears she could not wish to be his wife.

Tying up all the plot strands, Jane tells Rochester of her year with the Rivers family in Morton and of her relationship with St. John. She makes Rochester jealous by enumerating St. John's virtues after each of Rochester's attempts to diminish him. But as she teases Rochester this way she solidifies the assurance in herself that she loves Rochester devotedly and St. John not at all. Her proper service, she feels to the very depth of her being, is as Rochester's wife and not as God's missionary to people in India.

Slowly, after their marriage, Rochester begins to regain some sight in one eye, and when Jane hands him their first child to hold, he can see repeated in him his own once clear and bright black eyes. Rochester's ward, Adele, grows into a healthy and helpful English girl. Jane had continued to care for her, although she was often away at boarding school. Jane, in fact, removed her from the one to which Rochester had sent her when Jane left him. It was too much like the cruel Lowood Institution she attended. With both Mary and Diana Rivers, who each have married, she also remains friendly. St. John never marries but goes to India, and he writes to Jane occasionally, although he never directly refers to her marriage, hoping she is living a devout life. The missionary life is killing him, as Jane knew it would her.

Jane Eyre ends with what Jane assumes will be St. John's last letter before his death. "My Master has forewarned me. Daily He announces more distinctly,—'Surely I come quickly!' and hourly I more eagerly respond,—'Amen; even so come, Lord Jesus!'" It is, perhaps, a strange way to end the book, with such a strong focus on St. John and his Christian faith, when *Jane Eyre* has not been the story of St. John. It is the story of Jane Eyre and her journey from being an unloved rejected outcast to becoming the beloved wife of the man she adores and a benevolent force in the life of nearly everyone she encounters. She rejects St. John's call to selfless devotion in favor of self-fulfillment. There is, in addition, except for St. John's calling and Helen Burns' quietism, little in the book suggesting that a Christian vision of the world is paramount. Rochester is awed by the fact that at the same time he called out to Jane into the night, at his window in Ferndean, she heard that call as she stood wavering in the garden at Morton about whether to marry St. John. He praises God for this miracle of intuition. But even accepting his religious reading of the event, it draws a picture of a God who is not the taskmaster of St. John's theology. Rather God is the facilitator of communication between loving hearts. Certainly, the values Jane Eyre herself represents appear chiefly to be ethical, with a particular focus on self-reliance and duty to others.

Giving the final words of the book to St. John, thus suggests a contrast between the kind of dedication that self-assertively pursues the abnegation of the self, and the sort of dedication that seems to offer the self in service to the good of others but also draws to itself every gift it desires. Jane explains to Rochester "if ever I did a good deed in my life—if ever I thought a good thought—if ever I prayed a sincere and blameless prayer—if ever I wished a righteous wish,—I am rewarded now. To be your wife is, for me, to be as happy as I can be on earth." But he responds, "Because you delight in sacrifice." "Sacrifice!" she counters, "What do I sacrifice?

Famine for food, expectation for content. To be privileged to put my arms round what I value—to press my lips to what I love—to repose on what I trust: is that to make a sacrifice? If so, then certainly I delight in sacrifice."

Critical Views

JOHN MAYNARD ON JANE'S SEXUAL AWAKENING

The two perspectives Brontë offers on Jane's story, as one of betrayal and loss in the plot and of fear and withdrawal in the psychological action, run together in the analysis of her reaction. It takes the form of a further and extreme regression completing that already at work in the symbolic action. In it, Jane becomes simultaneously frozen by the betrayal and confirmed in her earlier frigidity. Brontë presents Jane's state after the failed wedding in a long, exceptionally rich and fine metaphorical description that reverses much of the seasonal and temporal motion of her life. Jane has become a "cold, solitary girl again" (p. 373) instead of an "ardent, expectant woman." The warm summer scene of her life and wedding has reverted to winter, creating a structural reversal of the scene in which her relationship with Rochester began. Her love is a child dying in a cold cradle, unable to get to Rochester's breast for comfort. The child that in Jane's dreams had seemed to image her attraction back away from marriage now seems to emblemize her hopeless regression. An allusion to the slaughter of the Egyptian first-born to describe her hopes—"struck with a subtle doom, such as, in one night, fell on all the first-born in the land of Egypt" (p. 374)—indirectly associates the entire chilling, killing process with a wrathful, repressive deity, an indication as well of the psychological forces at work in Jane. Having brought her back from girl to child, the imagery moves Jane's state further back to a final primal and primitive position. She is cut off from normal sensation—eyes covered and closed—and her inner experience seems a black and confused flow of eddying darkness. She abandons all will and feels as if she has laid herself down in a dried-up bed of a great river waiting for a flood to overwhelm her. We need not insist on dubious specific identifications of river bed with the birth passage or the waters with the amniotic fluid to recognize in this dark, sightless, turbulent, and watery place some of the

45

symbolic constants of primal experience. Jane longs for death in this total breakdown of personality and total regression and feels the floods come flowing over her.

Jane's breakdown fits her character as Brontë has drawn it to this point. The failure of her first approach to any adult relationship naturally sends her back to the cold, wet world of her detached childhood in which we find her at the opening. At the same time we are aware that the reaction is dangerous and indeed, for all the betrayal in Rochester's secret plan, excessive. The passage, one of the most impressive in the book, is also one of the most subjective. Jane's ice and snowstorm in summer is a winter scene most emphatically in the eye of the beholder. When she stops in the middle of her description to consider Rochester, we see that she is unable to be entirely fair to him. She is persuaded that he will try to expel her from Thornfield immediately. His feeling for her she judges not as real affection but as merely a "fitful passion: that was balked" (p. 374). He will want her no more. This judgment runs counter to everything we have seen of Rochester; immediately afterward we see how untrue it is to Rochester's future intentions, which are to stay with Jane, to be with Jane by any stratagem feasible. The characterization is more subtle than is generally appreciated. Brontë shows us Jane responding to loss in a way that is understandable and in language that allows us to share her inner experience. Yet she also exercises the care of a Jane Austen to show us how this motion away from sexual opening into a primal winter of the self also depends upon and creates a misjudgment of her situation. Jane is not loveless, only the victim of one more, much more serious act of manipulation by Rochester.

As Jane is forced to confront Rochester's continued desire for her at any price, on any terms, Brontë has the kind of opportunity her art so welcomes. Jane's psyche, like that of Elizabeth Hastings, can be explored *in extremis*. Her approach is something akin to nineteenth-century opera, where extreme situations are developed because they provide opportunities for a large and articulated display of essential emotional and psychological states. Jane continues to undergo a process of intense self-suppression. When she begins to have feelings of regret that she must leave Thornfield, she is forced back brutally by an act of conscience: "conscience, turned tyrant, held passion by the throat, told her, tauntingly, she had yet but dipped her dainty foot in the slough, and swore that with that arm of iron, he would thrust her down to unsounded depths of agony" (p. 379). The work of suppression is presented not as a rational triumph of conscience but as a threatening turmoil. In a great inner solitude and silence she hears the "ruthless" judge that haunts her mind proclaim Christ's unpsychiatric advice with a vengeance not in the Bible: "You shall, yourself, pluck out your right eye; yourself cut off your right hand: your heart shall be the victim; and you, the priest, to transfix it" (p. 379). Reeling from this reaction, Jane comes out of her room and falls—only to be caught by Rochester who has been faithfully awaiting her for hours. He carries her into the library, nourishes her with food, sits quite near her, warms and attracts her.

There follows a long scene that is essentially one in which the extremes of temptation and suppression are displayed at work in Jane. Close to the beginning of the scene, Rochester becomes so wrought up that Jane seriously fears that he will overpower her. He threatens that if she won't hear reason he will try violence. His own metaphor, of himself as a Samson about to break entanglements like tow, shows the limits of his power. He is ensnared by a woman; Jane feels no real fear and subdues him by reverting to tears. But soon Rochester's talk of a villa for two by the Mediterranean stirs his pulse once again. There then follows a fuller and more candid history of Rochester's sexual life, a story well calculated both to stir Jane's own sexual interest, as Rochester had earlier, and to win her sympathy for his lonely, unmated lot. We are aware at the same time that Jane has found a power to resist Rochester greater than that she ever had previously. Her "resolute, frozen look" (p. 386) is unendurable to him. He tries to rest his head on her shoulder; she refuses; he tries to draw her to him; she says no. She primly criticizes Rochester's mistressed life in Europe. Rochester's casual contempt for his mistresses leads

Jane to conclude that he would one day look upon her in the same way if she now yielded to him. Nothing in the story or his character justifies this conclusion, which, as much as moral issues, is the operative factor in her decision not to become his mistress. That is, distrust of Rochester motivates her as much as scruples about a relationship with a man technically married to a madwoman.

Nevertheless, when Rochester entreats her for a pledge of love Jane finds her attraction to him almost equals her resolution to renounce him. She experiences an ordeal, feels "a hand of fiery iron" (p. 402) grasp her vitals, undergoes a moment of struggle, blackness, burning. No one, she realizes, could love her better and she absolutely worships him. Yet one "drear word comprised my intolerable duty—'Depart!'" (p. 403). Jane's second crisis arrives at this moment. Rochester speaks to her with a gentle voice that yet turns her "stone-cold with ominous terror—for this still voice was the pant of a lion rising." As she keeps refusing him, he manages successively to bend toward her, to embrace her, to kiss forehead and cheek. When she extricates herself, he undergoes a wild look and rises, leaving Jane grasping the back of a chair for support. Inspired by her obvious need for it, Jane finds a language mostly unfamiliar to her, of belief in heaven and Victorian faith in striving and enduring against the temptation of "vice" and "lust" (p. 404).

Rochester's answer is a strong if entirely utilitarian one which few, if any, modern readers can resist: marriage is a human law; Jane's solitary position in the world allows her to do what she wants without hurting anyone. Jane finds the argument enticing and is driven to her extreme point of inner crisis. Even her reason and conscience now seem to side with her feelings and desires. Against all she asserts herself: "I care for myself. The more solitary, the more friendless, the more unsustained I am, the more I will respect myself" (p. 404). That self-respect is then defined in terms of consistency to laws and principles she has generally accepted before now. The point is important because it shows Jane, too, rather than being a rigid moralist after the zealots of the book, bases her ultimate morality on a standard relative to the individual. It is not that she couldn't disagree with convention, only that she disqualifies herself to do so under her present passion. Like Bertha, she is insane when sexually aroused, "insane—quite insane: with my veins running fire, and my heart beating faster than I can count its throbs" (p. 405). She will respect the dictates of her habitual self. The specific position puts Jane, within the novel's varying perspectives on the relative validity of sexual expression or suppression, in a stance of suspicion of sex. What is seen in a moment of passion is for that reason questionable; passion would seem to lead only to Bertha's kind of madness, not to new understanding. Jane could be true to herself by being true to her passionate self, but this is not a position that her present attitude toward sexual arousal will allow her to hold. Jane thus asserts her integrity by rejecting Rochester. Later, in a different relation to passion, she will accept him.

Rochester now approaches her a second time in a passion almost verging on rape: "His fury was wrought to the highest ... he crossed the floor and seized my arm, and grasped my waist. He seemed to devour me with his flaming glance: physically, I felt, at the moment, powerless as stubble exposed to the draught and glow of a furnace" (p. 405). However, he can do nothing. His passion subsides into noble rant about a noble bird in a cage. He might crush or tear the cage but would never obtain the inner self to which he also wishes to make love. He ends in a plea, "Oh! come, Jane, come!" then passes on to a "deep, strong sob" (p. 406). Jane pauses in her retreat to bless him, only to find his full passion vented upon her for the third and last time in this longest of temptation scenes: "Up the blood rushed to his face; forth flashed the fire from his eyes; erect he sprang: he held his arms out; but I evaded the embrace, and at once quitted the room" (p. 407). The entire scene has been dominated by these successive passionate drives of Rochester toward Jane, each one, except perhaps this last, provoking a stronger crisis in Jane. One can obviously find scenes of passion with a stronger physical presence, with more to arouse and involve the reader. But few can compare to this in the care with which Rochester's feeling is itself made credible and in the degree of sophistication with which Jane's complicated and very divided response is analyzed.

Jane has her dream that night of being back in the red-room at Gateshead; she takes the warning to flee temptation. She leaves as plain Jane Eyre, a girl driven by inner compulsion rather than a woman. Jane's account of her departure from Thornfield ends strangely in what is almost self-accusation at her compulsive departure. She abhors her "frantic effort of principle" (p. 410) and contrasts it to the lovely July natural order. She is hateful in her own eyes; yet she cannot turn back: "God must have led me on. As to my own will or conscience, impassioned grief had trampled one and stifled the other" (p. 410). God comes in here rather oddly. The entire passage has that strange confusion of tone we found in the narration of Caroline Vernon's seduction. The first person succeeds here—where the third person fails in the novelette—in rendering what may very well have been Brontë's own uncertainty as a complex reaction of the character herself. Some inner force—why not call it God—carries her away from Rochester's attraction. She is aware that it compels her above the normal motivations of conscience or conscious will. At such moments Jane falls into her occasional fictive mode of providential tale without persuading the reader that he is really reading myth rather than a psychologically revealing novel. The dramatic effect is to bring us into Jane's calamity: to feel all the pain and injury of her decision to depart even as we appreciate the strength of the inner necessity that she follows.

Brontë's success as a novelist in creating a character who seems to live for us both as a physical presence and in psychological depth is testified to by the very variety of interpretations that responsible critics have made of her leaving. For some she simply follows religion over desire; for others religion is merely an expedient to an act of self-will, or of necessary self-preservation against male authority; to others, as we have seen, Jane is driven by a deep-seated fear of incest or neurotic block at sexual initiation. What is clear is that with the fictional Jane, as with a complex situation in life, a variety of such factors are at work within, in an intricate configuration.

We see the failure of her sexual awakening not as a schematic reduction of experience but as a case study in careful analysis of the many vectors in a response to a highly wrought sexual situation. No simple reductive explanation will do. Jane leaves, driven by suppressive, super-ego-like domination; she also leaves racked by regret for the unnatural hurt she does Rochester; she also leaves almost overcome still by sexual desire. Indeed, she finds her hand gliding up involuntarily to the latch on Rochester's bedroom door as she slips away. Jane has been accused of being a castrator, but here the image that haunts her mind, of a prisoner passing nature indifferent as she goes to her own decapitation, surely suggests that the first victim of her compulsive need to flee Thornfield is her own sexual nature, which she hereby cuts out and renounces. Such a turmoil of feelings and reactions may not make simple interpretative schemas for critics or simple psychological case studies for amateur analysts. But it is the stuff of excellent novelistic art and Brontë has shaped it with fine craft.

Irene Tayler on Brontë's Heroines

We saw how at fourteen Charlotte depicted in "Albion and Marina" her own dilemma of wanting to be loved by her father yet also to be ambitious and accomplished like him. In that story Albion was torn between the values of domestic happiness at home with Marina and independent achievement out in the larger world, characterized by the "majestic charms" of Zenobia. The structural elements of this early story Charlotte retained in *Jane Eyre*, keeping them remarkably intact—but with two great transformations: first, the sex roles have been reversed; and second, the "Marina" of the novel is not dead at the end, only somewhat deadened.

The "Albion and Marina" framework enters *Jane Eyre* in midnovel, right after the interrupted false marriage. Jane and Rochester are avowed lovers, but Jane takes Albion's role and departs from a grieving Rochester to seek her way alone in the world. Moor House is not the fantasy land of Glasstown, but it does have its wish-fulfilling capacities, for there Jane comes into her own: finds a congenial family (in contrasting parallel to the Reeds), receives a large inheritance, and becomes, as she says, "an independent woman" (p. 556). St. John Rivers stands in the Zenobia spot, tempting Jane away from her first love and toward a competing ambition. As she wavers, Jane receives a supernatural call, and like Albion notes the time and acts on it instantly. Albion had found on his return not the joy of reunion but a "desolate and ruined apartment" and his beloved in the grave. Says Jane returning to Thornfield, "I looked with timorous joy towards a stately house: I saw a blackened ruin." The switch in sex roles that this parallel reveals is oddly underscored in the text of *Jane Eyre* itself. Presumably to prepare the reader for the shock of Thornfield's ruin and at the same time to build the suspense, Jane introduces her revelation with a digression that recalls the original story and gender roles which the novel has revised in retelling. Jane is seeking Rochester at Thornfield, but finds it demolished and empty. She describes her tender expectation and then the shock of horror that succeeds it.

> A lover finds his mistress asleep on a mossy bank; he wishes to catch a glimpse of her fair face without waking her. He steals softly over the grass, careful to make no sound; ... now his eyes anticipate the vision of beauty.... But ... how he starts! How he calls aloud a name.... He thought his love slept sweetly: he finds she is stone-dead.
>
> I looked with timorous joy towards a stately house: I saw a blackened ruin. (pp. 542–43)

Jane's first thought is that Rochester may be, like Marina, in the grave—"My eye involuntarily wandered to the grey church tower"—but he is not, though as he later tells her he "was forced to pass through the valley of the shadow of death" (p. 571). Rather, "one eye was knocked out, and one hand so crushed that Mr. Carter, the surgeon, had to amputate it directly" (p. 549). This is the biblical punishment for adultery; as many critics have noted, it amounts to symbolic castration.

How had Charlotte brought her original vision of the relative male and female conditions to this astonishing reversal? For Charlotte's early heroines the need for paternal love had to take precedence over any intellectual ambition, because their survival depended on it. The abandoned Marias could only die; even Zenobia was driven mad by Zamorna's rejection. But by the time of "Captain Henry Hastings," written in 1839 when she was turning twenty-three, Charlotte had strikingly strengthened her emotional position. She had recovered a new source of love in the mother figure "Hope," a moon and rainbow goddess evolved from Gray's vision of the "Mighty Mother" nature. And she had seen through her "genius" brother well enough to skewer him as the hangdog Henry Hastings. Now she could picture herself in the role of Henry's sister Elizabeth who literally arose amid maternal moonlight—"Resurgam"—from Rosamund Wellesley's grave to say goodbye to her lover and go her way free and alone. With this act Elizabeth both symbolically resurrected her feminine forebears (the human dimension of "mother") and became herself a model for future heroines, an early version of Jane Eyre repudiating the dishonorable proposals of the man she adored but to whom she would not surrender her integrity.

Elizabeth's assertive act is curiously encoded directly within *Jane Eyre*. Readers of the novel will recall that in the character of Helen Burns Charlotte depicted her mothering eldest sister Maria, whose death from an illness contracted at the Cowan Bridge school marked a nadir in young Charlotte's life. To Jane's masochistic assertion that "to gain some real affection" from one she loved, she would "willingly submit to have the bone of my arm broken, or to let a bull toss me, or to stand behind a kicking horse, and let it dash its hoofs at my chest" (all striking images of the destructive power of male sexuality), Helen mildly returns, "Hush, Jane! you think too much of the love of human beings" (pp. 80–81) and recommends instead the love of God. Acknowledging that her own father will not miss her when she is gone, Helen asserts that we have in heaven another and better "mighty home" (p. 67) presided over by a loving "Universal parent" (p. 96). Soon after, she dies in Jane's arms, a victim of Brocklehurst's oppression. The narrative of her story concludes:

> Her grave is in Brocklebridge churchyard: for fifteen years after her death, it was only covered by a grassy mound; but now a grey marble tablet marks the spot, inscribed with her name, and the word "Resurgam." (p. 97).

Presumably Jane herself supplied the marker. But its significance lies in the fact that it is Charlotte's own self-coded reminder of what she had already accomplished imaginatively, through her fiction, when in arising from Rosamund's grave and departing from her human lover, Elizabeth raised and redeemed the spirit of Maria Brontë, prototype of all Charlotte's fictional women who had "died of love."

The results of that resurrection permeate *Jane Eyre* and help account for Jane's successes. To begin with, we can now understand the ambiguous gender and meaning of Jane's visionary visitor in the red-room scene at Gateshead. Ostensibly the child fears the ghost of her uncle; but the vision she imagines has more the attributes of a remembered mother:

> I wiped my tears .... fearful lest any sign of violent grief might waken a preternatural voice to comfort me, or elicit from the gloom some haloed face, bending over me with strange pity.

Seeing a light gleam on her wall, Jane imagines it the "hearald of some coming vision from another world" and swoons to a "rushing of wings" (p. 15). Jane's collapse is painful, of course; but its practical result is to get her removed to Lowood, and on her way in life. Mother has risen—and helped.

At its next appearance the vision's gender, relationship, and purpose are made utterly explicit. As the grief-frozen Jane is struggling to convince herself to leave Rochester after the attempted false marriage, she sleeps and has a dream:

I dreamt I lay in the red-room at Gateshead; ... The light that long ago had struck me into syncope, recalled in this vision, seemed glidingly to mount the wall.... the gleam was such as the moon imparts to vapours she is about to sever. I watched her come.... She broke forth as never moon yet burst from cloud: ... then, not a moon, but a white human form shone in the azure, inclining a glorious brow earthward.... It spoke to my spirit: immeasurably distant was the tone, yet so near, it whispered in my heart—

"My daughter, flee temptation!"
"Mother, I will." (p. 407)

In departing, Jane is both an Elizabeth Hastings leaving William behind among the graves of women who have succumbed to male blandishments, and an Albion leaving (in Rochester) an anxious and abandoned Marina. "He would feel himself forsaken; his love rejected," muses Jane at the door; "he would suffer; perhaps grow desperate. I thought of this too ... and glided on" (pp. 408–9).

The story of Albion and Marina shows us that Rochester's maiming is in effect a commuted death sentence. Indeed in a sense one Rochester has died, and another taken his place. The earlier Rochester would have proved to be another Zamorna, whose love is doubly threatening. First, it fetters: as Jane tells us, echoing the Marys and Minas before her, Rochester's influence "took my feelings from my own power and fettered them in his" (p. 218). And then it carries always the covert threat of being withdrawn, with fatal results for the woman. Jane remarks later as she looks back on the wisdom of her escape, "oh, yes, he would have loved me well for a while ..." (p. 459). Over this Zamorna type Jane has triumphed, with mother's help, by exchanging roles and leaving him behind to die the death of Marina.

The Rochester Jane marries is in that sense a different man: Zamorna shorn of his power to endanger women is no longer really a Zamorna, but rather the male equivalent of Jane herself insofar as she is a loyal, loving, intelligent companion. He is now pretty much bereft of his dazzling sexual magnetism, but at the same time he will never depart. Their life together could almost be that of contented father and daughter. In fact their union has been arranged and blessed by mother herself—a curious circumstance that I shall return to in a moment.

Anita Levy Contrasts Jane, Blanche, and Bertha

What then would a more fully historicized reading of personal experience as represented in and by Brontë's novel look like? In provisional answer, we must return to the question embedded in Gaskell's tale of Brontë in the dressing room—what information constitutes a nineteenth-century woman's novel? A reading of several scenes may provide a brief history of fiction to account for the "experience" the novel is made of, and that which it in turn makes. Jane's conversation with a perplexed Mrs. Fairfax, as the exasperated governess tries to determine exactly what her new master is made of, lends itself particularly well to this project.

"Is Mr. Rochester an exacting, fastidious sort of man?"

"Not particularly so; but he has a gentleman's tastes and habits, and he expects to have things managed in conformity with them."

"Do you like him? Is he generally liked?"

"Oh, yes; the family have always been respected here. Almost all the land in the neighborhood, as far as you can see, has belonged to the Rochesters time out of mind."

"Well, but leaving his land out of the question, do you like him? Is he liked for himself?"

"I have no cause to do otherwise than like him; and I believe he is considered a just and liberal landlord by his tenants: but he has never lived amongst them."

"But he has no peculiarities? What, in short, is his character?"

"Oh! his character is unimpeachable, I suppose. He is rather peculiar, perhaps: he has travelled a great deal, and seen a great deal of the world, I should think. I dare say he is clever: but I never had much conversation with him."

"In what way is he peculiar?"

"I don't know—it is not easy to describe—nothing striking, but you feel it when he speaks to you; you cannot be always sure ... whether he is pleased or the contrary: ... but that is of no consequence, he is a very good master."[20]

The exchange, or rather miscommunication, between Jane and Mrs. Fairfax opposes two kinds of information about what makes a human being human, or in other words, competing semiotic models for interpreting personal experience. Jane attempts to extract information from the housekeeper about Rochester, the unique personality. She inquires after his idiosyncrasies, his attractiveness to Others, his innate appeal, his peculiarities, and, finally, his "character." Mrs. Fairfax replies with information about property, kinship relations, and social standing. Rochester is, above all, an aristocratic male— landed, well traveled, and master of all he surveys. His features, in this model, are common among men of his estate. Jane, of course, is far from satisfied with the housekeeper's replies to her insistent questions. "This was all the account I got from Mrs. Fairfax of her employer and mine," she complains (136), thereby screening out a wealth of social and cultural information in a move that Ward might call narrowing down.[21]

To understand more precisely the discursive operations of the two models just described, compare Mrs. Fairfax's description of Blanche Ingram, Mr. Rochester's bride-to-be, with Jane's. The housekeeper draws the following portrait of the queenly Miss Ingram: "'Tall, fine bust, sloping shoulders; long graceful neck; olive complexion, dark and clear; noble features.... And then she had such a fine head of hair, raven-black, and so becomingly arranged; a crown of thick plaits behind, and in front the longest, the glossiest curls I ever saw. She was dressed in pure white; an amber-coloured scarf was passed over her shoulder and across her breast, tied at the side, and descending in long, fringed ends below the knee. She wore an amber-coloured flower, too, in her hair: it contrasted well with the jetty mass of her curls'" (Brontë, 189). In addition to her beauty, Blanche is greatly admired for her "accomplishments," especially her singing skills.

Mrs. Fairfax's description represents the aristocratic woman as a collection of attributes located on the surface of the body. Miss Ingram is little else than superficial characteristics and social accomplishments lacking depth and interiority. The female body, so depicted, is an iconic or pictorial body, a display of power similar to that of Queen Elizabeth's ornately decorated surface in the famous Ditchley portrait, now gracing the cover of the Norton Anthology of English Literature.[22] But when Jane glimpses Blanche, she describes the same features very differently. "She was very showy, but she was not genuine; she had a fine person, many brilliant attainments, but her mind was poor, her heart barren by nature; nothing bloomed spontaneously on that soil; no unforced natural fruit delighted by its freshness" (Brontë, 215). The first part of each statement takes sociocultural information, Mrs. Fairfax's discourse, and redefines it as information about the surface that is therefore superficial. The second half of the statement inserts information about the person herself, or personal information.

It is tempting, no doubt, to attribute Jane's response to her jealousy and insecurity. Yet one could just as easily say that here Brontë is rethinking or reimagining what makes a woman desirable and using her experience to validate a whole new class of people. Specifically, the very characteristics that should make the aristocratic Blanche attractive as a wife—beauty, accomplishments, money, and property—become negative features of the female individual. What has actually been rendered unattractive here is the aristocratic female, who, by all rights, should be desirable precisely for her looks, property, and blood. An opposing idea is constructed of the "normal" female who carries certain qualities around within her body. Supposedly, these features are independent of wealth, land, or family connections, relying instead on an innate self possessing unique assets superior to mere externals such as wealth or beauty. Jane Eyre, of course, lacks these traditional resources and yet proves to be the most highly prized of women. In contrast, the aristocratic woman is "barren," bears no "natural fruit," and lacks "freshness" and spontaneous bloom, presumably lacking the "depths" for these things to take root. The images of nature indicate the existence of a natural self prior and more essential to sexual identity than any mere social construction.[23]

Through yet another such gesture of displacement, the madwoman first paces the attic and then attacks her master: "In the deep shade, at the farther end of the room, a figure ran backwards and forwards. What it was, whether beast or human being, one could not, at first sight tell: it grovelled, seemingly on all fours; it snatched and growled like some strange wild animal: but it was covered with clothing, and a quantity of dark, grizzled hair, wild as a mane, hid its head and face." In her primal state she "was a big woman, in stature almost equaling her husband, and corpulent besides: she showed virile force in the contest—more than once she almost throttled him, athletic as he was" (Brontë, 321). Woman, so represented, violates the boundaries between categories; animal/human, male/female, genders and generations all combine in one figure of undecidability.[24] Like the so-called primitive females anatomized by nineteenth-century anthropologists and medical men, her sexuality is in excess, overwhelming her gender and almost overwhelming that of her husband.[25] Several passages from nineteenth-century sociology and anthropology demonstrate that what is preverbal, presocial, and yet most basic to the self is yet another layer of writing. According to Italian criminologist Cesare Lombroso, the lower-class prostitute "is disguised by youth with its absence of wrinkles and the plumpness which conceals the size of the jaw and cheekbones, thus softening the masculine and savage features."[26] English physical anthropologists William Flower and James Murie represent the nature woman, like the lower-class one, as lacking in properly gendered features: "The clitoris [is] of moderate size, but with a well-developed prepuce, and far more conspicuously situated than in the European female."[27] Femaleness, so represented, is either too little (the prostitute's masculine features) or too much (the Bushwoman's

59

overdetermined genitals), both making the woman unfemale. Brontë made Bertha Mason out of the same language early-nineteenth-century sociology used to justify new restrictions on working-class women and anthropology to justify their scientific studies of African women.[28]

Jane appears to discover in the extra chamber of Rochester's house the wife he married for her fortune and brought home from the West Indies years earlier. What is produced is a psychologically determined notion of female experience. With the discovery of Bertha Mason's presence, sexual scandal becomes the ultimate secret at the very center of mansion, narrative, and individual. Beneath all Rochester's sexual adventures Jane uncovers the far greater scandal of an arranged marriage that precludes the possibility of a companionate relationship between them. Jane, therefore, takes on value as a woman by virtue of having neither a rich exterior nor barbarous ungendered depths. By means of this double negative, Brontë produces a new nature so displayed in Jane's relationship with Rochester at Ferndean: "There was no harassing restraint, no repressing of glee and vivacity with him; for with him I was at perfect ease, because I knew I suited him; all I said or did seemed either to console or revive him. Delightful consciousness! It brought to life and light my whole nature: in his presence I thoroughly lived; and he lived in mine" (Brontë, 461). Such nature is neither based in mere physical presence, since blind Rochester cannot even see Jane's body, nor in sexual passion, which is degenitalized in favor of Jane's capacities as companion and nurse. Female experience with depth displaying itself on the surface in the quality of female consciousness becomes synonymous with experience itself.

Notes

20. Brontë, *Jane Eyre* (1847; rpt. New York: Penguin, 1985), 136.

21. Fiction of the 1840s like *Jane Eyre*, *Wuthering Heights*, and *Mary Barton* laid claim to innate powers of common sense, decency, and morality on behalf of the individual and by extension for an entire group of people. Only in so doing could those without ancient aristocratic prerogatives to power, specifically property or blood, claim for themselves the right to say what was human and natural

about human nature and so assert their superior individuality. On this point see Armstrong (n. 6).

22. For a discussion of the history of the iconic, aristocratic body see Leonard Tennenhouse, *Power on Display: The Politics of Shakespeare's Genres* (New York: Methuen, 1986).

23. Such gestures within fiction exposing the falsity of social identity are also common in feminist theory, as Judith P. Butler contends in *Gender Trouble: Feminism and the Subversion of Identity* (New York: Routledge, 1990).

24. Blanche Ingram, like Bertha Mason, bears a certain physical similarity to Rochester. She has "eyes rather like Mr. Rochester, large and black," and like him, she is tall and dark (Brontë, 189). Neither Rochester's wealthy fiancée nor his first wife is sufficiently gendered to enact the exchange demanded by the terms of the companionate marriage that ends the novel. Both, moreover, are represented in highly orientalized terms.

25. On the semiotic overlap of race and gender tropes in nineteenth-century anthropology see Anita Levy, *Other Women: The Writing of Class, Race, and Gender, 1832–1898* (Princeton, N.J.: Princeton University Press, 1991).

26. Cesare Lombroso and William Ferrero, *The Female Offender* (London: T. Fisher Unwin, 1895), 97; emphasis added.

27. Flower and Murie, "Account of the Dissection of a Bushwoman," *Journal of Anatomy and Physiology* 1 (1867): 207.

28. On the restrictions placed upon working-class women see Judith Walkowitz, *Prostitution and Victorian Society: Women, Class, and the State* (Oxford: Oxford University Press, 1980).

JOHN G. PETERS ON JANE'S OTHERNESS

Throughout the novel, Jane appears as a threat to the other characters. Either because she is an intruder from outside the community, because she is an enigma, or because her ideas are threatening, the other characters marginalize Jane in order to dismiss her or her ideas and thereby transform her into something non-threatening. From the very outset, the characters exclude Jane; even as a child she is isolated from the social group:

Eliza, John, and Georgiana were now clustered round their mama in the drawing-room ... Me, she had dispensed from joining the group; saying, "She regretted to be under the necessity of keeping me at a distance; but that until she heard from Bessie, and could discover by her own observation that I was endeavouring in good earnest to acquire a more sociable and child-like disposition, a more attractive and sprightly manner,—something lighter, franker, more natural as it were—she really must exclude me from privileges intended only for contented, happy little children."[1]

This scene is indicative of Jane's situation at Gateshead, and her otherness in relation to the Reeds remains unchanged throughout the novel. Even later at her aunt's deathbed, Jane says of Mrs. Reed, "Poor, suffering woman! it was too late for her to make now the effort to change her habitual frame of mind: living, she had ever hated me—dying, she must hate me still" (p. 242). Gateshead becomes representative of Jane's position outside the social order as a whole.

Except for those at Lowood and Marsh End (who are also social outsiders in part), the other characters in *Jane Eyre* generally exclude Jane from their social spheres, and they do so in various ways. For example, John Reed says to Jane, "You have no business to take our books: you are a dependent, mama says; ... you ought to beg, and not live here with gentlemen's children like us, and eat the same meals we do, and wear clothes at our mama's expense" (p. 11). He wants to separate Jane from himself by removing from her some of the outward signs of their similarity. Similarly, Mrs. Reed also marginalizes Jane; Jane recalls, "[S]ince my illness she [Mrs. Reed] had drawn a more marked line of separation than ever between me and her own children; appointing me to a small closet to sleep in by myself, condemning me to take my meals alone, and pass all my time in the nursery while my cousins were constantly in the drawing-room" (pp. 26–27). By separating Jane from her own children, Mrs. Reed removes her from the Reeds' social group, placing Jane instead among the servants. And when Jane falls ill during the red-room incident, Mrs. Reed sends for Mr. Lloyd, an apothecary, who was "sometimes called in by

Mrs. Reed when the servants were ailing: for herself and the children she employed a physician" (p. 19). In this way, Mrs. Reed marks a clear distinction between her own children and Jane by lumping Jane with the servants. But the servants will not have Jane either; Miss Abbot says, "No; you are less than a servant, for you do nothing for your keep" (p. 12). So Jane is not allowed inside either community.

Even outside Gateshead, Jane continues to exist as the other. Soon after she arrives at Lowood, Brocklehurst attempts to exclude Jane from the society of the school; he places her on a stool and tells the inhabitants that Jane "is a little castaway: not a member of the true flock, but evidently an interloper and an alien" (p. 67). He then advises: "You must be on your guard against her; you must shun her example: if necessary, avoid her company, exclude her from your sports, and shut her out from your converse" (p. 67). By his choice of "interloper" and "alien" (words Jane also used to describe Mrs. Reed's view of her), Brocklehurst tries to transform her into the other and then urges those of the school to reject Jane if they wish to remain members of the larger social group.

Jane is shunned in a like manner when she arrives in Morton. Not only do the inhabitants treat her as an outsider because she is one but also because she does not fit into any recognizable category. She begs food but is not a beggar. She looks like a lady but has no money. When she offers to trade belongings for food, they rebuff her. When she seeks employment, they answer her evasively. When she seeks out the clergyman, he is unavailable. When she attempts to gain entrance to the Rivers' home, Hannah, both literally and symbolically, shuts the door on her. As a result, the isolation she experiences when she first arrives there is more than simply a spiritual isolation; she is literally shut out from all aspects of life until St. John finally takes her into the Rivers' home.

Even at Thornfield, by the very nature of her being a governess, she does not easily fit into the established roles of either gentry or servants. As a governess, she is a dependent; yet she is better born and better bred than the other servants. Only Mrs. Fairfax is of the same social group, but their differences of age and interests make them merely superficial companions. As far as her relationship to the gentry is concerned, the way the Ingram party relegates Jane to the category of governesses (whom they considered to be completely outside their social group) also emphasizes Jane's place outside the social sphere at Thornfield. Blanche Ingram says of governesses, "I have just one word to say of the whole tribe: they are a nuisance" (p. 179). She then goes on to describe the Ingrams' vicious treatment of them when they were children. And Blanche's mother says, "[D]on't mention governesses: the word makes me nervous. I have suffered a martyrdom from their incompetency and caprice: I thank Heaven I have now done with them!" (p. 179). Then specifically aiming her remark at Jane, she says, "I see all the faults of her class" (p. 179). So, as at Gateshead, Jane fits neither among the gentry nor among the servants.

In order for Jane to appear outside the community, the characters must actively exclude her, and among the various ways the characters transform Jane into the other, the labels and imagery with which they describe her are the most subtle, poignant, and effective.[2] These labels consistently depict Jane as non-human. Others call her "angel," "cat," "sprite," "imp," "thing," "rat," and "fairy"—to name just a few. In fact, such terms appear nearly a hundred times in the novel, and given their sheer frequency alone, they are more than merely incidental.

Early in the novel, characters describe Jane almost exclusively with derogatory labels. And by so doing, they marginalize Jane. When the Reeds call her an "imp" or a "rat," they both punish her by the insult and psychologically isolate her from their family. These terms also reinforce for the Reeds the goodness of their family by excluding an "imp" or "rat" from their community. Jane's otherness at Gateshead culminates in the red-room incident. Immediately after they call her "rat" and "mad cat," they thrust Jane into the red-room, a tomb-like room they had left undisturbed since Mr. Reed's death. This symbolic interment and the labels they use on Jane represent the physical and spiritual solitary confinement to which the Reeds relegate her. Jane's transformation into the other is important for the Reeds, because if they can think of Jane as an animal or creature, then they can treat her as non-family (in opposition to Mr. Reed's deathbed request [p. 240]). A retrospective Jane understands her position; she says she was "an interloper not of her [Mrs. Reed's] race, and unconnected with her" (p. 16). During her feverish, deathbed ravings, Mrs. Reed reveals her motivation in excluding Jane from their community:

Such a burden to be left on my hands—and so much annoyance as she caused me, daily and hourly, with her incomprehensible disposition, and her sudden fits of temper, and her continual, unnatural watchings of one's movements! I declare she talked to me once like something mad, or like a fiend—no child ever spoke or looked as she did: I was glad to get her away from the house ... I hated it [Jane] the first time I set eyes on it—a sickly, whining, pining thing! It would wail in its cradle all night long—not screaming heartily like any other child, but whimpering and moaning. Reed pitied it; and he used to nurse it and notice it as if it had been his own: more, indeed, than he ever noticed his own at that age. (pp. 233–34)

Here, Mrs. Reed excludes Jane not only from her own family, but also from the human family as well. In this brief passage, she calls Jane "unnatural," "fiend," "thing," "beggar," "creature," and finally "it," thus emphasizing her relationship to Jane. Equally clear is the reason for Mrs. Reed's attitude: Jane represents a threat to her aunt's family. When Mrs. Reed says her husband used to "notice it [Jane] as if it had been his own: more indeed, than he ever noticed his own at that age," she expresses the unspoken concern that Jane is usurping the place of her own children. Mrs. Reed's natural protective instinct toward her children takes over, and she attempts to rid the family of Jane's ties to it. Her attitude toward Jane also sheds light on Mrs. Reed's withholding of John Eyre's letter. She suggests she acts out of vengeance (which is true), but she also keeps Jane from joining her class through Jane's becoming a financial equal; as long as Jane remains financially dependent she remains both outside the Reed's family and outside their social circle.

Separating the other from society is perhaps the oldest and most basic of acts against those we regard as enemies. By transforming the enemy into something other than human in our minds, we can treat them other than humanely—thereby avoiding guilt and possible retribution. Rene Girard, in speaking of scapegoats, says:

> All our sacrificial victims, whether chosen from one of the human categories ... or, a fortiori, from the animal realm, are invariably distinguishable from the nonsacrificeable beings by one essential characteristic: between these victims and the community a crucial social link is missing, so they can be exposed to violence without fear of reprisal. Their death does not automatically entail an act of vengeance.[3]

Of course, Jane functions less as a scapegoat at Gateshead than she does as the other (although she does refer to herself as "the scape-goat of the nursery" [p. 16]), but the underlying principle is the same. By transforming Jane into the other—an animal, creature, or non-entity—her aunt avoids the guilt of crimes against her family and social group. Mrs. Reed divests Jane of human, family, or social ties that could claim retribution.[4] Consequently, Mrs. Reed has no fear of reprisal from conscience or from other people and in fact can view herself and her behavior positively, in that she removes a threat to her family and society.

Besides the possibility of Jane's usurping her own children's place, Jane's fiery temper and strength also threaten Mrs. Reed. These characteristics challenge Mrs. Reed's authority as head of the family and as a member of the ruling class; they also threaten to influence the Reed children. In addition, Jane exposes the Reeds' selfishness and uncharitability. This becomes particularly important, because the Reeds represent the ruling class as a whole. As a result, although Jane's threat as a child is primarily limited to the Reeds, on a larger scale, her challenge to their authority also implies a challenge to the society and class they represent. This becomes clear as Jane grows and continues to challenge cultural norms concerning the role of women and class in society. Brocklehurst recognizes this threat to the Reeds and to society and says to those at Lowood, "[A]t last her excellent patroness [Mrs. Reed] was obliged to separate her [Jane] from her own young ones, fearful lest her vicious example should contaminate their purity" (p. 67). With Jane marginalized, Mrs. Reed can ship her off to Lowood and then relinquish "all interference in [Jane's] affairs" (p. 90).

Transforming a person into the other through labeling also occurs elsewhere in the novel. For example, Blanche Ingram calls Jane a "creeping creature" (p. 225). Whether Blanche does this because she senses Rochester's interest in Jane, because of her opinion of governesses in general, or because of class snobbery, the result is the same: she relegates Jane to a position outside at least the social community if not outside the human community entirely. Similarly, Blanche refers to Adele as a "tiresome monkey" (p. 191), and Rochester calls Adele a "French floweret" (p. 141). In both cases, they dismiss Adele by using an epithet. And even though Rochester appears to have some affection for the child, he often dismisses her as superficial and insignificant. Jane herself also uses this tactic; when John Reed attacks her, she turns him into a "murderer," "slave-driver," and "Roman emperor" (p. 11). He seems to understand the implications of this transformation when he replies, "What! what! Did she say that to me? Did you hear her, Eliza and Georgiana?" (p. 11). And this in part accounts for Jane's assertion to Helen that she could never love or bless him (p. 58), since in Jane's mind he is the other. As she does with John Reed, Jane also wishes to sever ties with Mrs. Reed when she says, "I am glad you are no relation of mine: I will never call you aunt again as long as I live" (pp. 36–37). In this case, the withholding of the label then transforms her aunt into a non-relation. And of course Rochester consistently uses this method to rid himself of his ties to Bertha. By calling her a "maniac" (p.304), a "demon" (p. 296), a "monster" (p. 313), and a "fiend" (p. 304), by referring to her "wolfish cries" (p. 312) and "demon-hate" (p. 312), by designating her attic room as "the mouth of Hell" (p. 296), and by otherwise describing Bertha using animalistic or non-human terms, Rochester tries to divest her of humanity in order to free himself from her. His marginalizing of Bertha through labeling culminates when he says, "For a wife I have but the maniac up-stairs: as well might you refer me to some corpse in yonder churchyard" (p. 320). The transformation now complete, Rochester then feels free to "form what new tie" (p. 313) he chooses.

Besides others marginalizing Jane through labeling, she sometimes does this to herself as well. She labels herself playfully with Rochester at times, but early on her self-marginalization is potentially tragic. The most poignant example is when she looks into the mirror in the red-room and thinks:

> [T]he strange little figure there gazing at me, with a white face and arms specking the gloom, and glittering eyes of fear moving where all else was still, had the effect of a real spirit: I thought it like one of the tiny phantoms, half fairy, half imp, Bessie's evening stories represented as coming out of lone, ferny dells in moors. (p. 14)

This passage couples the loneliness and isolation of Jane with the otherworldly, non-human description of her image (appropriate for the red-room). Her visualization is representative of her spiritual situation. For Jane, because of her age and child-like impressionability along with the constant labeling by the Reeds, becomes in her own mind as well a "phantom" or "imp." She sees herself moving through Gateshead either ignored or attacked and at all points an outsider—ultimately even to herself.

Although as Jane grows older, she rejects more and more the labels assigned her, even as an adult she occasionally marginalizes herself through labeling. When Jane chastises herself for thinking Rochester could possibly favor her, she calls herself, "Blind puppy!" (p. 163). Jane aligns herself with the non-human world, both as punishment and as explanation for her unusual belief that one of Rochester's class could consider Jane worthy of notice. And soon after arriving in Morton, Jane refers to her broken heart as being "impotent as a bird with both wings broken" (p. 328). At this time when Jane feels most isolated from those around her, most outside every social community, she again labels herself with terminology from the non-human world.

The role then of negative labels is plain enough in their transforming Jane into a social outsider, but there are just as many positive terms describing Jane. For example, among other things, she is called "angel," "fairy," "dove," and "genii." But regardless of whether the labels are positive or negative, their function is the same: that is, they marginalize Jane from the community, because in the minds of those who label her, she must be transformed into something other than human.

Rochester uses the majority of these eulogistic terms, and he also, like so many others, wishes to marginalize Jane. Even though he loves Jane, he clearly believes in the traditional role of women in the nineteenth-century social order, and part of this view is the idea of woman as idol.[5] In order to worship Jane, however, he must first make her other than mere mortal. By calling her "angel" and "fairy," he separates her from other people and lifts her onto a pedestal. Jane fully understands the implications of this position and consistently rejects Rochester's attempts to turn her into what she is not. For example, when Rochester calls Jane an angel, she says, "I am not an angel" (p. 262); elsewhere she says, "Don't address me as if I were a beauty: I am your plain, Quakerish governess" (p. 261). And after Rochester threatens to dress Jane in fine clothes and jewels, she says, "And then you won't know me, sir; and I shall not be your Jane Eyre any longer, but an ape in a harlequin's jacket,—a jay in borrowed plumes" (pp. 261–62). Jane's use here of "ape," "harlequin," and "jay" shows she recognizes that to change her as Rochester wishes would transform her into something she is not. And Jane wishes to be neither sub-human nor super-human.

Similarly, Rochester uses non-human terms for Jane (even his eulogisms) because she is an enigma to him, as she is for St. John later and for society in general. Some are threatened by this; others are merely puzzled. Those at Gateshead (except Bessie) consistently find Jane different from most children. Abbot says, "I never saw a girl of her age with so much cover" (p. 12), and Mrs. Reed says, "[T]here is something truly forbidding in a child taking up her elders in that manner" (pp. 7–8). At Gateshead, Jane's difference is threatening. However, others merely see Jane as unusual. Bessie says to Jane, "You are a strange child ... a little roving, solitary thing ... [Y]ou're such a queer, frightened, shy little thing" (p. 39). St. John says to her, "You are original" (p. 379). And Rochester implies the same, when he says to her, "[A]ny other woman would have been melted to marrow at hearing such stanzas crooned in her praise" (p. 276). Rochester often cannot understand Jane's ideas or actions, and if she becomes for him (even if unconsciously) other than mortal, then he need not consider the implications of her views. Yet Jane simply wants to be thought of as a normal human being. And this attitude is precisely the problem, in that her assertion of equality threatens to take her out of the nineteenth-century feminine role of subservience in a male-dominated world.[6]

To twentieth-century readers, the threatening character of the novel is less apparent. But clearly such was not true for many of Brontë's time. For example, when Jane claims equal status with the Ingrams, based not on birth or wealth but rather on character, she rejects the usual criteria for evaluating class. In fact, at one point, she even claims a superiority to Blanche: "Miss Ingram was a mark beneath jealousy: she was too inferior to excite the feeling" (p. 187). And when Jane thinks Rochester "is not of their [the Ingram's] kind. I believe he is of mine;—I am sure he is ... though rank and wealth sever us widely, I have something in my brain and heart, in my blood and nerves, that assimilates me mentally to him" (p. 177), she again asserts her equality based on character, not birth, and rejects the usual criteria for determining a mate. Similarly, when Jane says, "[W]omen feel just as men feel; they need exercise for their faculties, and a field for their efforts as much as their brothers do; they suffer from too rigid a restraint, too absolute a stagnation, precisely as men would suffer" (p. 110), she questions the traditional roles of women, again asserting an equality based on character, not birth. In each instance, she threatens established social norms. And despite the fact that Jane's views ostensibly only affect her own life, she carries the seeds of change, and the implied changes represented by Jane's actions are unusually troubling to those of her time—both inside the novel and outside it.[7] As evidenced by the virulence of some of the negative contemporary reviewers of *Jane Eyre*, many perceived Jane and the novel to be subverting social, political, and religious norms. For example, Jane's strength of character and will along with her refusal to be forced into a submissive position seem very masculine. Rochester says, "Jane, be still; don't struggle so, like a wild, frantic bird that is rending its own plumage in its desperation." Jane replies, "I am no bird; and no net ensnares me: I am a free human being with an independent will; which I now exert to leave you" (p. 256). Rochester tries to type Jane as a bird, but she rejects this label and insists on human status. He likes Jane's fiery strength, but for him Jane is a "bird" or a "fairy" at those times. If he were to think of her as a woman asserting her independence, then his position as sole master would be threatened. Consequently, even though Rochester's motives in marginalizing Jane are not malicious (as are the Reeds' and the Ingrams'), as is true for many of the characters in the novel, Rochester can deal more easily with Jane if he can view her as other than normal.

Despite the fact that Rochester accepts the traditional role of nineteenth-century women, he does not fit the stereotypical mold of the nineteenth-century male. His openness concerning his continental affairs, his willingness to engage in bigamy, and his desire to marry a woman so far below his social standing all show that Rochester rejects many of the social conventions of his day, and his willingness to move outside the social mores explains why his relationship with Jane becomes possible.

One of the effects of Rochester's flouting social customs and Jane's marginalization is the curious influence it has on the rapport between them. As Rochester becomes more and more interested in developing a romance with Jane, he begins more and more to use terms of animal and supernatural imagery to describe himself. He calls himself "devil" (p. 263), "ogre" (p. 273), "ghoul" (p. 273), "dog" (p. 451), "toad" (p. 307), and "ape" (p. 307), among other things. And since Rochester has already come to view Jane as a "bird" and "fairy" (and so on), his self-labeling moves him into the non-human world inhabited by Jane and thus allows in his mind (and perhaps in hers as well) for the progression of their relationship, because Jane too picks up this labeling; she says Rochester's hair is "raven-black" (p. 436) and that he is a "fierce falcon" (p. 192), a "wild-beast or bird" (p. 436), a "caged eagle" (p. 436), a "demon" (p. 284), and "phantom-like" (p. 281), so that finally, as a consequence of this labeling, they begin to inhabit the same world. Once their engagement occurs, Rochester says, "[W]herever I stamped my hoof, your sylph's foot shall step also" (p. 262). And when Jane returns to him (in a sense sealing their engagement), she says, "[Y]ou talk of my being a fairy; but, I am sure, you are more like a brownie" (p. 443). Later, she continues this idea when she says that Rochester is like "a royal eagle, chained to a perch, ... forced to entreat a sparrow to become its purveyor" (p. 444). At this point in the novel, they realize they are different, and they both become inhabitants of the non-human world, a world where their relationship finally comes to fruition.

Ultimately, this labeling becomes more than merely metaphoric and affects the conclusion of the novel. Certainly, Rochester's injuries from the fire are necessary to humble him, bring him to religious susceptibility, reduce his power, and make Jane more his equal; however, his physical disabilities also move him visibly away from his position as a "normal" member of society. In fact, at Ferndean, he actively seeks isolation from other people. Mary says to Jane late in the novel, "I don't think he will see you. He refuses everybody" (p. 437). And this isolation then qualifies him to engage in a relationship with Jane. He, like Jane, becomes, in part at least, the other—because of his mutilation, his reclusive behavior, and the non-human labels used on him. Consequently, he moves more literally into Jane's sphere outside social boundaries.

As a result of all this, the rather out-of-the-ordinary relationship between Jane and Rochester becomes both possible and non-threatening to society. Of course, they are not social lepers, but they are unusual, and they seem to fit each other—and perhaps no one else. John says of the match, "She'll happen do better for him nor ony o' t' grand ladies" (p. 455). And earlier in the novel, after leaving Rochester, Jane herself feels she could marry no one but him. Also amply implied is that had Jane not returned Rochester never would have married. Consequently, their relationship at the close of the novel is much better than it would have been had they married earlier as originally planned.

Notes

1. Charlotte Brontë, *Jane Eyre*, ed. Margaret Smith (Oxford: Oxford Univ. Press, 1980), p. 7. Hereafter, all quotations from *Jane Eyre* will be taken from this edition and will be followed by their page numbers in parenthesis.

2. Lynn Hamilton ("Nicknames, Forms of Address, and Alias in Jane Eyre," *Literary Onomastics Studies* 14 [1987]: 69–80) suggests, "Nicknames in Jane Eyre function not only to indicate relation but also to reflect the protagonist's initial isolation and her transition out of isolation into relation and community" (p.76). However, I disagree with Hamilton and will argue that the labeling used on Jane always serves to transform her into the other and that there is no real "transition out of isolation into relation and community." At the close of the novel, Jane is still isolated from all those except her family.

3. Rene Girard, *Violence and the Sacred*, trans. Patrick Gregory (Baltimore: The Johns Hopkins Univ. Press, 1977), p. 13.

4. Jane recognizes this when she remarks that Mrs. Reed "was resolved to consider me bad to the last: because to believe me good, would give her no generous pleasure: only a sense of mortification" (p. 233).

5. See, for example, John Ruskin's popular essay "Of Queen's Gardens."

6. In recent years, many critics have noted aspects of gender and gender equality in Jane Eyre. See, for example, Eva Figes, *Patriarchal Attitudes* (New York: Stein and Day, 1970. pp. 157–63: Adrienne Rich, "Jane Eyre: The Temptations of a Motherless Woman," *Ms.* 2 October

1973): 69–72+; Carolyn Heilbrun, *Toward a Recognition of Androgyny* (New York: Alfred A. Knopf, 1973), pp. 58–59; Ellen Moers, *Literary Women* (Garden City, NY: Doubleday & Company, 1976), pp. 15–20; Nancy Pell, "Resistance, Rebellion, and Marriage: The Economics of Jane Eyre," *Nineteenth-Century Fiction* 31 (March 1977), pp. 397–420; Sandra M. Gilbert and Susan Gubar, *The Madwoman in the Attic* (New Haven: Yale Univ. Press, 1979), pp.336–71; Margaret Miller, "Happily Ever After: Marriage in Charlotte Brontë's Novels," *Massachusetts Studies* in English 8.2 (1982): 21–38; Elaine Showalter, *A Literature of Their Own: British Women Novelists from Brontë to Lessing* (London: Virago Press, 1982), pp. 100–32; and Cynthia Carlton-Ford, "Intimacy without Immolation: Fire in Jane Eyre," *Women's Studies* 15 (1988): 375–86.

7. There has been some debate as to whether *Jane Eyre* suggests any real changes in social, political, or gender issues. See, for example, Robert Bernard Martin, *The Accents of Persuasion: Charlotte Brontë's Novels* (New York: W. W. Norton & Company, 1966), p. 93; Jina Politi, "Jane Eyre Class-ified," *Literature and History*, 8 (Spring 1982): 56–66; Gayatri Chakravorty Spivak, "Three Women's Texts and a Critique of Imperialism," *Critical Inquiry*, 12 (Autumn 1985): 243–61; Valerie Grosvenor Myer, *Charlotte Brontë: Truculent Spirit* (London: Vision Press, 1987), p. 113; and Parama Roy, "Unaccommodated Women and the Poetics of Property in Jane Eyre," *Studies in English Literature 1500–1900*, 29 (Autumn 1989): 713–27. To one degree or another, these critics all suggest that Jane does not actually subvert traditional norms but rather reinforces those norms. However, whether this is true or not is irrelevant to the fact that the characters in the novel and the contemporary negative reviewers of the novel perceive Jane to be subversive.

LAWRENCE J. STARZYK ON THE SIGNIFICANCE OF PICTURES

At two critical moments, first when Jane contemplates leaving Lowood and next as she settles in as governess at Thornfield, Jane finds a vantage point from which to regard her still unrealized prospects. Following Miss Temple's marriage and departure from Lowood, Jane meditates on the "transforming process" (100) that occurs as she must now put off all she had borrowed from her teacher and become intellectually independent. Her choice of vantage point is significant.

I went to my window, opened, and looked out. There were the two wings of the building; there was the garden; there were the skirts of Lowood; there was the hilly horizon. My eye passed all other objects to rest on those most remote, the blue peaks: it was those I longed to surmount; all within their boundary of rock and heath seemed prison-ground, exile limits. I traced the right road winding round the base of one mountain, and vanishing in a gorge between two: how I longed to follow it further. (100–101)

The Tennysonian aspiration of pursuing an ever-vanishing horizon, the Macaulayan gospel of inevitable progress inform Jane's ambitions here and elsewhere in the novel: she is a true Victorian. She is also the quintessential romantic, a figure, like many of Caspar David Friedrich's, who stand over against the universe. Like Friedrich's "Woman at a window," like Arnold's speaker in "Dover Beach," Jane engages the world before her from the protective security afforded by the framing window from which she looks. As she approaches the window, she recalls "that the real world [unlike the limited Lowood] was wide" (100).

A critical discontinuity evidences itself in this moment when Jane enthusiastically embraces the distant prospect of the "real" while simultaneously remaining secure from whatever threats it poses. This Friedrich-like picture fails to acknowledge the artist in the present recollecting this event from her past. Jane's autobiography permits a complex narrative stance from which discrete temporal occurrences ultimately must be regarded as confused. The self, which in the past securely gazed upon a distant prospect of indefinable promise or peril, is now looked upon in the present by its self. The young governess, framed by the window and contemplating her self as Rochester's wife, indicates a principal function of the pictorial in Jane's world: the comparison of impressions wrought in historical moments with the "ideal stores" of personality from which they derive.[7]

A similar meditation on a distant prospect occurs when Jane settles in at Thornfield. Shortly after arriving at Rochester's castle, Jane follows Mrs. Fairfax to the third floor. The tapestry- and portrait-lined hall had the appearance of a "shrine of memory." This corridor provides access to the battlements to which Jane regularly retreats when not absorbed in her teaching duties. Her "sole relief" from her responsibilities, where she could feel "safe in the silence and solitude of the spot and allow my mind's eye to dwell on whatever bright visions rose before it," the castle leads provide more than a diversionary vision of the landscape opening before her. Along the battlements, Jane confesses, "I longed for a power of vision which might overpass that limit; which might reach the busy world, towns, regions full of life I had learned of but never seen: that then I desired more of practical experience than I possessed; more of intercourse with my kind, of acquaintance with variety of character, than was here within my reach." Here, within the regions of the "mind's eye" and "inward ear," Jane casts a "tale that was never ended—a tale my imagination created, and narrated continuously; quickened with all of incident, life, fire, feeling that I desired and had not in my actual existence" (132). At this point in her meditation, Jane contemplates how confining her existence at Thornfield is and how limitless appear the prospects for personal growth and development in a world of infinite possibilities. The juxtaposition of these conflicting portraits allows Jane vicariously to attenuate her actual situation without, however, exposing herself to the possible threats existing within the limitless view she sees from the leads.

But Jane's imaginative landscapes are not merely temporary and naive palliatives. During a conversation following their aborted marriage, Rochester interprets Jane's countenance as shrewdly evidencing the inefficacy of such abstractions. Jane's features, as Rochester reads them, seem to be saying, "My fine visions are all very well, but I must not forget they are absolutely unreal. I have a rosy sky, and a green flowery Eden in my brain; but without, I am perfectly aware, lies at my feet a rough road to travel, and around me gather black tempests to encounter" (399–400). Jane's three water colors depict how tempestuous reality can be and how unlike her imaginative world is the Eden ostensibly figured before her mind's eye. The prescience of Rochester's interpretation of Jane's countenance begins to reveal the real motive informing Jane's fascination with the pictorial and with the juxtaposition of "bodily impressions" and the images of the brain from which they derive. To a woman who, throughout her story, protests against being "a discord" (13), a "solitary" (80), who finds fundamental discontinuity between her self-portraits and her paintings of others (most notably Miss Ingram), who discovers that "she is not worthy of notice" (27), existence is not a matter of being "where there was life and movement" (105), but in finding a companionable form, a likeness attesting to essential equivalency with an other. All of her paintings, whether actual or imagined, betray the absence of such equivalency. Rochester alone provides it; twice he acknowledges her as his "likeness" (319, 328). And Jane, in her earliest recollections of the man who becomes her "idol" (346, 403), admits to taking keen delight in "imagining the new pictures he portrayed" (180).[8]

This affinity of spirit, however, is as ineffective a palliative as Jane's Edenic musings. Shortly before she confesses her delight in Rochester's portraitures, the master of Thornfield warns his governess of the narrowness of vision she herself freely admits to in her distanced perspective on the wide world. "You think all existence lapses in as quiet a flow as that in which your youth has hitherto slid away," Rochester admonishes her in words providing a telling gloss on the water colors he recently examined.

> Floating on with closed eyes and muffled ears, you neither see the rock bristling not far off in the bed of the flood, nor hear the breakers boil at their base. But I tell you— and you may mark my words—you will come some day to a craggy pass of the channel where the whole of life's stream will be broken up into whirl and tumult, foam and noise: either you will be dashed to atoms on crag points, or lifted up and borne on by some master wave into a calmer current. (174–75)

Rochester's admonition coincides with Jane's desire to engage the "real" world that exists beyond the limiting confines of Lowood and Thornfield. And it recognizes the inherent danger possible in such engagement. What is intriguing about Rochester's common-sense warning is that his portrayal of Jane's situation and its possible resolutions coincide remarkably with the water colors he examined two chapters earlier. Jane is predestined, in her own mind and in Rochester's warning, either to founder perilously among rocks and crags, where she will either succumb, like the "half-submerged mast," and become "a drowned corpse" floating in green water, or to sit triumphantly like the woman "crowned with a star" amid the reflections of the Evening Star.[9] Either resolution derives from the encounter with a "colossal head" resting against an iceberg, whose defining features include "a brow quite bloodless, white as bone, and an eye hollow and fixed, blank of meaning but for the glassiness of despair" (153).

Herein lie the portraits of Rochester and St. John Rivers confused.[10] Jane's real predicament involves discerning which constitutes her likeness and redemption. That she discriminates between the two in resolving the existential dilemma represented by her watercolors becomes clear when, at novel's end, she returns to Rochester. The fallen figure with hollowed eye allows himself to be unwittingly teased into jealousy as Jane describes her relationship with St. John Rivers, the cold, glacial figure with "Grecian profile" who rationally attempts to coerce Jane into missionary submission. "'The picture you have just drawn'" Rochester tells Jane, "'is suggestive of a rather too overwhelming contrast. Your words have delineated very prettily a graceful Apollo: he is present to your imagination,— tall, fair, blue-eyed, and with a Grecian profile. Your eyes dwell on a Vulcan,—a real blacksmith, brown, broad-shouldered, and blind and lame into the bargain'" (565). The gods of fire and light contend in Rochester's analysis for victory over Jane. But the second watercolor depicting the triumph of the Evening Star makes clear to all but the blind Haephestus that the contest has been prejudiced in his favor.[11]

Even before encountering Rochester for the first time, Jane admits to an aesthetic bias privileging the dark. Walking toward the post office in Hay, Jane hears in the distant night the sounds of a horse coming toward her. The "metallic clatter" of the horse's trappings "effaced the soft wave-wanderings" of the nearby stream. In a striking analogy intended to explain this acoustic effacement, Jane resorts, as is frequently her wont, to the visual. "As, in a picture, the solid mass of a crag, or the rough boles of a great oak, drawn in dark and strong on the foreground, efface the aerial distance of azure hill, sunny horizon, and blended clouds, where tint melts into tint" (135). The pictorial analogy is fascinating for a number of reasons, not the least of which is its revelation of Jane's innate tendency, even in the literary genre she employs to tell her story, to revert to the visual when attempting to explain the auditory.[12] Jane's concern that her artistic attempts to embody shadowy forms or ideas invariably attest to human inadequacy is reinforced by this analogy which reconfirms Jane's difficulty in rendering effable the pictures housed in memory.

Notes

7. Jane's analysis of the red-room scene becomes paradigmatic of this significant bifurcation. In the "visionary hollow" of the bedroom mirror, she sees "a strange little figure there gazing at me, with a white face and arms specking the gloom" (12). Rather than an example of Jane's total self-involvement from which, according to Blom, she regards others as "adjuncts or impediments to her own fulfillment" (104), such moments in which the divided self manifests itself must believed as indicative of the process of development Jane engages in. The self must encounter its self as "other" first before recognizing the essential companionableness of that "strange figure."

8. This kinship Jane repeatedly experiences in the presence of Rochester supports Rich's contention that Jane's marriage to Rochester is a "continuation of this woman's creation of herself" (106).

9. Meditating on Rochester's deception, Jane describes herself as "self-abandoned.... I seemed to have laid me down in the dried-up bed of a great river. I heard a flood loosened in remote mountains, and felt the torrent come" (374).

10. All of the critical assessments of Jane's portfolio paintings referenced above (Gates, Langford, McLaughlin) argue temporal discriminations in quintessential elements where no distinctions exist.

11. For a detailed discussion of the significance of the Evening Star and moon for Jane, see Heilman.

12. Tromley insightfully remarks that "So often do scenes echo paintings that we begin to suspect we are dealing with canvas rather than the printed page" (47).

MICAEL M. CLARKE COMPARES JANE TO CINDERELLA

Jane Eyre echoes the German *Cinderella* in many ways. A brief survey will demonstrate how skillfully Brontë evokes the tale's central symbol—the hearth. Welcoming hearths, for example, signify the precious caregiving qualities associated with the hearthkeepers. Miss Temple's hearth provides the first home for Jane's intellect and spirit, and this sacred space is illuminated by the moon, also traditionally associated with female deities: "Some heavy clouds, swept from the sky by a rising wind, had left the moon bare; and her light, streaming in through a window near, shone full both on us and on the approaching figure, which we at once recognised as Miss Temple ... [Her apartment] contained a good fire, and looked cheerful" (chap. 8, p. 61). Gradually, Brontë expands on this "good fire": "The refreshing meal, the brilliant fire, the presence and kindness of her beloved instructress ... had roused [Helen Burns's] powers within her. They woke, they kindled: first, they glowed in the bright tint of her cheek ... then they shone in the liquid lustre of her eyes ... which had suddenly acquired ... radiance" (chap. 8, p. 63).

Every homecoming in this novel is associated with a hearth and domestic caretaking: at Thornfield, Mrs. Fairfax in her "snowy muslin apron," with her knitting and her cat, welcomes Jane Eyre to her "snug, small room; a round table by a cheerful fire" with an invitation, "you must be cold; come to the fire" (chap. 11, p. 83). When Jane returns to visit her dying aunt at Gateshead, Bessie, the one person in the Reed household who had treated Jane kindly and the source of her knowledge of fairy tales, presides in a lodge that is "very clean and neat: the ornamental windows were hung with little white curtains; the floor was spotless; the grate and fire-irons were burnished bright, and the fire burnt clear" (chap. 21, p. 199). In Brontë's private history, Bessie bears a close resemblance to "Tabby," the kindly servant who, after Charlotte's mother's death, fed the children generously and, in Winifred Gerin's words, "cared for their frail bodies."[10]

David Lodge points out that *Jane Eyre* "contains about eighty-five references to domestic fires" as well as some dozen references to hearths, about forty-three figurative and ten literal references to fire, and four to hell-fire. In *Jane Eyre*, Lodge demonstrates, Brontë conveys "a very significant cluster of emotions and values" by means of fire imagery, developed and expanded with remarkable fluidity from literal description into lyrical evocations of passionate and spiritual states of being.[11]

At Moor House, the hearth represents family, intellectual companionship, emotional intimacy, and even life itself, as a shivering, exhausted, and starving Jane looks in from the outer cold and darkness on a "room with a sanded floor, clean scoured; a dresser of walnut, with pewter plates ranged in rows, reflecting the redness and radiance of a glowing peat-fire." Near the hearth, "amidst the rosy peace and warmth," sit two "young graceful women—ladies in every point." Their faces look "thoughtful almost to severity," and yet, Jane feels, "I seemed intimate with every lineament" (chap. 28, pp. 292–3). Like Miss Temple's, their names are significant: Mary and Diana represent Christian and mythical figures who symbolize female chastity and integrity. On the other hand, Rochester's "bed of fire" makes clear that the domestic embers may be fanned into the demonic, uncontrolled fires of a mad wife's rage, and Helen Burns (her name indicates Brontë's deliberateness), who has "only a father ... and he will not miss me," dies by a fever signifying the destructive quality of self-abnegation that is preached to women by Christian ministers such as Brocklehurst and St. John Rivers (chap. 9, p. 71). Thus, hearthfire in *Jane Eyre* represents all that is needful, desired, and inspiring, but also that which has a terrifying potential for devastation and destruction.

And what of the saintly mother in heaven? Brontë takes this invisible but actively intervening figure from the Grimms' tale and transforms her into an image that resonates with powerful echoes of ancient female deities, especially that of the moon-goddess. In doing so, she defies conventional expectations that the novel be realistic and presents a supernatural figure straight out of the Grimms' *Cinderella*: a mother in heaven who watches over, guides, and inspires Jane in crucial moments.

Moon imagery is essential to *Jane Eyre*. Not only does the moon shine full on Miss Temple in the passage quoted above, it is also clearly associated with Jane's mother in the scene in which Jane struggles to decide whether to stay with Rochester after learning that his mad wife still lives. Jane falls asleep and dreams of the moon breaking through clouds:

> a hand first penetrated the sable folds and waved them away; then, not a moon, but a white human form shone in the azure, inclining a glorious brow earthward. It gazed and gazed and gazed on me. It spoke to my spirit: immeasurably distant was the tone, yet so near, it whispered in my heart—"My daughter, flee temptation!"
> "Mother, I will."
> (chap. 27, p. 281)

The moon also illuminates Jane's first doubts about Christian teachings: "the moon rose with such majesty in the grave east ... And then my mind made its first earnest effort to comprehend what had been infused into it concerning heaven and hell: and for the first time it recoiled, baffled" (chap. 9, p.69).

Moonlight "streamed through the narrow window near my crib," it brightens and gleams on Jane's first meeting with Rochester, "her glorious gaze" rouses Jane Eyre just before Bertha's first attack, and illuminates Jane's declaration of love and independence (chap. 5, p. 34). Rochester, too, remarks the effect of the moonlight, as he reminds Jane that she "glowed in the cool moonlight last night, when you mutinied against fate, and claimed your rank as my equal" (chap. 25, p. 230). In every case, Brontë associates the moon with a kind of sacred presence.

Before the abortive marriage ceremony, the moon foreshadows Jane's isolation and suffering. On the eve of Jane's intended wedding, the moon's "disk was blood-red and half overcast; she seemed to throw on me one bewildered, dreary glance, and buried herself again instantly in the deep rift of cloud." Soon afterward, she "shut herself wholly within her chamber, and drew close her curtain of dense cloud; the night grew dark; rain came driving fast on the gale" (chap. 25, pp. 243–4). But that very night, after Bertha Mason's visit to Jane Eyre's room, during which she rips the bridal veil, the moon once again "shone peacefully," as if relieved, having warned her daughter (chap. 25, p. 251).

Again and again, Brontë uses these symbols—the hearth and the moon—to represent a heavenly mother and virgin moon-goddess, offering Jane Eyre a spiritual integrity lacking in the version of Christianity represented by Brocklehurst and St. John Rivers.

After St. John Rivers has insisted that Jane Eyre marry him, for propriety's sake, and so that he would be possessed of "a wife: the sole helpmeet I can influence efficiently in life and retain absolutely till death," the moon again plays a decisive role in Jane's peril of soul (chap. 34, p. 357): "I contended with my inward dimness of vision, before which clouds yet rolled. I sincerely, deeply, fervently longed to do what was right; and only that. 'Show me, show me the path!' I entreated ... All the house was still ... the room was full of moonlight. My heart beat fast and thick; I heard its throb. Suddenly, it stood still to an inexpressible feeling that thrilled it through, and passed at once to my head and extremities ... I saw nothing: but I heard a voice somewhere cry—'Jane! Jane! Jane!' nothing more" (chap. 35, p. 369, emphasis added).

Again Jane has had a vision, described in terms that stretch the limits of the realistic novel and that is a religious, rather than a gothic, element. It is related to the conversion experience so typical of Victorian autobiography—in this case a woman's conversion experience:

I broke from St. John, who would have followed, and would have detained me. It was my time to assume ascendancy. My powers were in play, and in force. I told him to forbear question or remark; I desired him to leave me: I must, and would be alone. He obeyed at once. Where there is energy to command well enough, obedience never fails. I mounted to my chamber; locked myself in; fell on my knees; and prayed in my way—a different way to St. John's, but effective in its own fashion. I seemed to penetrate very near a Mighty Spirit; and my soul rushed out in gratitude at His feet. I rose from the thanksgiving—took a resolve—and lay down, unscared, enlightened-eager but for the daylight. (chap. 35, p. 370)

(...)

Like Cinderella, Jane Eyre runs away from the too-powerful prince, though others sell themselves daily to such men, even, step-sister-like, deforming themselves in a vain attempt to meet their requirements. The issue between Jane Eyre and Edward Rochester after the interrupted marriage ceremony and revelation of Bertha Mason's existence is not so much Rochester's deception, nor the moral question concerning his still-living wife, as it is a question of male power versus female integrity. This has been the issue between them from the first.

Although Jane Eyre is attracted by Rochester's strength of character, she fears it in a world where men are encouraged to misuse their power. From the very beginning, Jane's wariness, her sometimes prickly independence, her bantering replies to Rochester, and her refusal to accept his gifts establish power as a key issue between them. And indeed, Rochester has long abused his privileges: as a young man, he married for money, using women for sex but wishing to possess them exclusively with no obligations in return. He is a distant domestic despot who mocks the feminine qualities of his ward Adele and forms no close attachments but lies to and teases women mercilessly. Yet, he is much admired and sought after in society. To paraphrase Oscar Wilde, that is all that need be said about society.

The scene—moonlit, of course—that leads to their engagement is filled with the language of equality: Jane's emotion asserts its "right to predominate," her spirit addresses his, "equal—as we are!" and he responds that "My bride is here ... because my equal is here" (chap. 23, p. 223). Shortly thereafter, when Rochester has informed Mrs. Fairfax of their plans to marry, she begins a litany of warnings on the theme of inequality: "He is a proud man," "Equality of position and fortune is often advisable ... He might almost be your father," and, "Try and keep Mr. Rochester at a distance ... Gentlemen in his station are not accustomed to marry their governesses" (chap. 24, pp. 232–3).

Most telling of all is Rochester's resort to threats of violence when he realizes that his deception will not work and that he may be balked of his desires: "'Jane! will you hear reason?... because, if you won't, I'll try violence ... Jane, I am not a gentle-tempered man ... beware!' ... his still voice was the pant of a lion rising." Brontë makes the underlying issue clear when Jane responds to Rochester's "It would not be wicked to love me" with "It would to obey you" (chap. 27, p. 278).

Jane Eyre's humble social position has, like Cinderella's, a double function. As emblems of unjust limitations placed on women, Jane's poverty and her life of service as under-housekeeper, governess, and teacher offer a social critique of women's subjection. But Brontë also asserts the worth of women's work. Its value is suggested by the many images of domestic peace and intellectual and spiritual nourishment offered by women at their hearthsides. Such service, if performed freely, is noble, and promotes good in others.

In the larger pattern of the novel, at the hearths of Miss Temple, Bessie, Mrs. Fairfax, and Mary and Diana Rivers, domesticity is associated with resistance to the life-denying principles of a tainted social system and with a spirituality that is not anti-Christian, but that seeks to reintegrate ancient maternalist principles into the Christianity that Brontë's father and his curates preached. Had the hearthkeepers more power,

Brontë seems to say, the Jane Eyres of the world could fulfill their ambitions and their desire for freedom.

In a letter to Elizabeth Gaskell dated 27 August 1850, Brontë wrote:

> Men begin to regard the position of women in another light than they used to do; and a few men, whose sympathies are fine and whose sense of justice is strong, think and speak of it with a candor that commands my admiration. They say, however—and, to an extent truly—that the amelioration of our condition depends on ourselves. Certainly there are evils which our own efforts will best reach; but as certainly there are other evils—deep-rooted in the foundations of the social system—which no efforts of ours can touch; of which we cannot complain; of which it is advisable not too often to think.[18]

Distinctive as he is in his Byronic attractiveness, Rochester is part of a larger pattern of masculine dominance: vide John Reed, the Rev. Brocklehurst, and St. John Rivers. At the center of this dominance is a displacement of the rightful relations between men and women by a religious system that places man between woman and heaven. Jane Eyre reflects: "My future husband was becoming to me my whole world; and more than the world; almost my hope of heaven. He stood between me and every thought of religion, as an eclipse intervenes between man and the broad sun. I could not, in those days, see God for his creature: of whom I had made an idol" (chap. 25, p. 241).

Women, by contrast, either become ruthlessly competitive and pettily cruel (Georgiana Reed, Mrs. Reed, and Blanche Ingram), having, in effect, cut off a part of themselves to please men, or they are swallowed up by a world that does not value them (Helen Burns and Miss Temple), as Cinderella fears will happen to her. The third alternative, and "the choice of life" for women, is that represented by the hearth, a "sacred space" where Cinderella's spirit is nourished through divine help, and where loving service brings joy. The hearth represents a place where women can, in Virginia Woolf's words, "look past

[John] Milton's bogey, for no human being should shut out the view."[19]

This book is neither a simple expression of female rage (though there is anger in it), nor a capitulation to the devalued female roles of nurse and servant. It is, rather, an expression of a maternalist system of values that was known and debated in Brontë's lifetime.[20] Nineteenth-century maternalists such as J. J. Bachofen, Friedrich Engels, Elizabeth Cady Stanton, and Charlotte Perkins Gilman believed that human society evolved through a number of stages, and that it was not always patriarchal.[21] Some, like Walter Bagehot, believed that woman, whose maternal instinct he considered the source of all altruism, provided the foundation of civilization.

Although Bachofen considered patriarchy superior to matriarchy on the scale of human social development, nineteenth-century feminists saw hope in the maternalist denial of the universality of female subordination: it suggested that equality between the sexes might be the more "natural" form of social organization, positing alternatives for women. And, in the nineteenth century, archeological evidence of mother-goddess figures was deployed for a variety of purposes, sometimes to support theories of the moral superiority of women, sometimes to argue, as did Sydney Owenson, Lady Morgan, in *Woman and Her Master* (1840), that woman's rightful place in human history had been hidden and suppressed by historians in order to keep women in subjection.

Maternalism offered an alternative vision of relations between the sexes to nineteenth-century thinkers and writers such as Brontë and William Makepeace Thackeray. That such ideas were not foreign to Brontë is demonstrated in *Shirley*, when Caroline Helstone and Shirley Keeldar, sitting in the churchyard while, within the church, "curates ... hammer over their prepared orations," discuss "what Eve was when she and Adam stood alone on earth." And what Eve was, was not Milton's Eve, for he "tried to see the first woman; but ... It was his cook he saw." Rather the first Eve, as Shirley describes her, was "heaven-born," "vast," "grand," "a woman-Titan" "Jehovah's daughter," an "undying, mighty being" who yielded the "unexhausted life and uncorrupted excellence ... which, after millenniums of crimes ... could conceive and bring forth a Messiah."[22] That Brontë would give the heroine who was based on her beloved sister Emily such words and ideas strongly suggests that Brontë herself found them compelling.

Cinderella's virtues then, the ethos she represents, are exactly those that the Victorians held to be peculiarly women's virtues, and Brontë's use of the tale in *Jane Eyre* represents a fusing of the German variant's mother-goddess implications with certain nineteenth-century ideas concerning human evolution and altruism as a female principle. Like the *Cinderella* tale, the novel is structured upon two competing religious systems, one female-centered and pre-Christian, the other patriarchal and Christian. It is only when the two are viewed together that we can understand Brontë's particular dialectic of fierce independence and romantic, seemingly antifeminist, ideas about women, duty, and altruistic caretaking.

The structure of *Jane Eyre* is a complex fusion of classical mythology, Christian allegory, and fairy tale, resulting finally in a feminist allegory, a woman's *Pilgrim's Progress*, in which those elements of Christianity that demean women's intelligence, will, desire, and integrity are assessed and found wanting. Brontë's is a Christianity reclaimed by the (re)insertion of a maternalist respect for women's work. In *Jane Eyre*, Brontë was able to reconcile grief for a lost mother and ambivalence toward the religion of her father. And it is the insertion into the novel of the Grimm Brothers' *Cinderella*, with its resonances of the supernatural and the mythic, that conveys this feminist ethic.[23]

Notes

10. Winifred Gerin, *Charlotte Brontë: The Evolution of Genius* (Oxford: Clarendon Press, 1967), pp. 34–9.

11. David Lodge, "Fire and Eyre: Charlotte Brontë's War of Earthly Elements," in *The Language of Fiction: Essays in Criticism and Verbal Analysis of the English Novel* (London: Routledge and Kegan Paul, 1966), pp. 114–43,116–7.

18. Elizabeth Gaskell, *The Life of Charlotte Brontë*, ed. and with an intro, by Angus Easson (Oxford: Oxford Univ. Press, 1996), p. 356. The reference to "a few men ... whose sense of justice is strong" surely

refers to William Makepeace Thackeray, whom Brontë praises so strongly in the preface to the second edition of *Jane Eyre*.

19. Virginia Woolf, *A Room of One's Own* (New York: Harcourt Brace Jovanovich, 1929), p. 118.

20. See especially Johann Jakob Bachofen's *Myth, Religion, and mother-Right* (1861), also Sydney Owenson, *Lady Morgan's Woman and Her Master*, Charlotte Perkins Gilman's *Women and Economics* (1861), Herbert Spencer's *Principles of Sociology* (1876–1896), Walter Bagehot's *Physics and Politics* (1869), Friedrich Engels's *Origin of the Family* (1871), Eleanor Marx's *The Woman Question* (1887), Mona Caird's *The Morality of Marriage* (1897), and Frances Swiney's *The Awakening of Women: Or, Women's Part in Evolution* (1897). I am indebted to Florence Boos's discussion of the ideological axes of agreement and difference among these and other writers in her "A History of Their Own: Late Nineteenth-Century Feminist Family History," delivered before the Midwest Victorian Studies Association in April of 1992. Gerda Lerner discusses the problematic yet influential workings of the ideas of matriarchy and maternalism in "Origins," in *The Creation of Patriarchy* (New York and Oxford: Oxford Univ. Press, 1986), pp. 15–35.

21. Lerner, p. 26.

22. Brontë, *Shirley* (Oxford: Clarendon Press, 1979), book 2, chap. 7, pp. 319–21.

23. Marianne Thormahlen's recent study, *The Brontës and Religion* (Cambridge: Cambridge Univ. Press, 1999), appeared after this essay had been written. Thormahlen's analysis is compatible with the views expressed here, in that she demonstrates that a "radical enquiry into religious thought, feeling, and conduct" characterizes all the Brontë works (p. 219). Moreover, she correctly represents Charlotte's critique of Anglicanism as a sign, not of rejection of the church, but of a loving desire to reform it. Thormahlen's study is to be commended for its impressive demonstration of the need for greater contemporary appreciation of the role of religion in nineteenth-century literature.

Thormahlen's study, however, focuses on the extent to which Christian institutions and ideas inform the Brontë novels, while my purpose is to show that in *Jane Eyre* Charlotte Brontë includes religious elements that range beyond those provided by Christianity alone.

Works by Charlotte Brontë

Novels

Jane Eyre, 1847.

Shirley: A Tale, 1849.

Villette, 1853.

Poetry

Poems of Currer, Acton and Ellis Bell, 1846.

Posthumous Publications

The Green Dwarf, 1833 (published 2003).

The Professor: A Tale, 1846 (published 1857).

The Twelve Adventurers: And Other Stories, 1925.

Legends of Angria, 1933.

Tales from Angria, 1954.

Early Writings of Charlotte Brontë, 1826–1832, 1987.

Early Writings of Charlotte Brontë, 1833–1834, 1991.

Early Writings of Charlotte Brontë, 1834–1835, 1991.

The Belgian Essays, 1996.

The Letters of Charlotte Brontë: 1848–1851. With a Selection of Letters by Family and Friends, 2000.

# Annotated Bibliography

Barker, Juliet. *The Brontës*. New York: St. Martin's Press, 1994.

Baker's volume is a comprehensive biography of a thousand pages of the Brontë family as individuals and in relation to each other and their Victorian context.

Beattie, Valerie. "The Mystery at Thornfield: Representations of Madness in *Jane Eyre*." *Studies in the Novel*, 28:4 (Winter 1996), pp. 493 (13).

Beattie argues that Bertha Mason, Rochester's insane wife confined to the attic in *Jane Eyre*, although an illustration of how patriarchal authority treats rebellious females, is not a powerless figure but, in her madness, a rebel against the limitations imposed on women in the nineteenth century.

Beaty, Jerome. *Misreading* Jane Eyre: *A Postformalist Paradigm*. Ohio State University Press: Columbus, 1996.

Beaty approaches the problem of interpreting *Jane Eyre* by examining the narrative, psychic, and social forces that organize the reader's experience of the work.

Bellis, Peter. "In the Window-seat: Vision and Power in *Jane Eyre*." *English Literary History* 54 (1987), pp. 639–652.

Focusing on the importance of seeing, Bellis argues that the relationship between Jane and Rochester is defined by conflicting, masculine and feminine, ways of looking at things.

Bossche, Chris R. Vanden. "What did Jane Eyre Do? Ideology, Agency, Class and the Novel." *Narrative* 13:1 (Jan 2005), pp. 46 (21).

Bossche discusses the ideological content of *Jane Eyre*, arguing that Jane expresses a radical ideology devoted to liberty and social inclusion.

Chen, Chih-Ping. "'Am I a Monster?': Jane Eyre among the Shadows of Freaks." *Studies in the Novel*, 34:4 (Winter 2002), pp. 367 (18).

Chen surveys the attitude of the Victorian English to what were considered alien or abnormal human forms and the recurrence of such forms in *Jane Eyre* and how they function in the novel.

Essaka, Joshua. "'Almost My Hope of Heaven': Idolatry and Messianic Symbolism in Charlotte Brontë's *Jane Eyre*." *Philological Quarterly*, 81: 1 (Winter 2002), pp. 81 (27).

Essaka argues that *Jane Eyre* is a profoundly Christian novel which emphasizes the importance of not using other people as Messiah figures in the hope of finding salvation through them, but still realizes the importance of human relationships.

Gilbert, Sandra M., and Susan Gubar. *The Madwoman in the Attic*. New Haven and London: Yale University Press, 1979.

Using Brontë's image of a confined madwoman as a controlling idea, Gilbert and Gubar analyze nineteenth-century fiction written by women, with an emphasis on Brontë's, focusing on how it subverts the authority of a male-defined social order.

Gordon, Lyndall. *Charlotte Brontë: A Passionate Life*. Chatto & Windus: London, 1994.

A biography of Charlotte Brontë focused on the strength of her character despite the gender expectations of her time and on the way she used and transformed events in her life into literature.

Heilman, Robert. "Charlotte Brontë's 'New Gothic,'" in R.C. Rathburn and M. Steinman, Jr. (eds), *From Jane Austen to Joseph Conrad*. Minneapolis: University of Minnesota Press, 1958.

Heilman argues that Brontë uses Gothic devices in *Jane Eyre* in order to examine and represent psychological events and social practices.

Imlay, Elizabeth. *Charlotte Brontë and the Mysteries of Love: Myth and Allegory in* Jane Eyre. St. Martin's Press: New York, 1989.

Imlay examines *Jane Eyre* through an analysis of archetypal mythic, folkloric and allegorical elements it contains.

Lamonaca, Maria. "Jane's Crown of Thorns: Feminism and Christianity in *Jane Eyre*." *Studies in the Novel*, 34:3 (Fall 2002), pp. 245 (19).

Beginning with the last lines of *Jane Eyre*, St. John Rivers' last letter, Lamonaca considers the role that Christianity as a determining belief system plays in the novel.

Nestor, Pauline. *Charlotte Brontë's* Jane Eyre. Harvester/ Wheatsheaf: New York, London, 1992.

Nestor provides a reading of the text focusing on its treatment of the ideas of motherhood, sexuality and identity.

Spark, Muriel. *The Essence of the Brontës*. Peter Owen: London & Chester Springs, PA, 1993.

This volume is a collection of Spark's writings on the Brontës along with a selection of the family's letters.

Vander Weele, Michael. "*Jane Eyre* and the Tradition of Self Assertion: or, Brontë's Socialization of Schiller's 'Play Aesthetic.'" *Renascence: Essays on Values in Literature*, 57:1 (Fall 2004), pp. 5 (24).

Vander Weele considers the nature and significance of acts of self-assertion in *Jane Eyre* and their relation to the struggle between passion and reason in the government of human behavior.

Contributors

Harold Bloom is Sterling Professor of the Humanities at Yale University. He is the author of 30 books, including *Shelley's Mythmaking, The Visionary Company, Blake's Apocalypse, Yeats, A Map of Misreading, Kabbalah and Criticism, Agon: Toward a Theory of Revisionism, The American Religion, The Western Canon,* and *Omens of Millennium: The Gnosis of Angels, Dreams, and Resurrection. The Anxiety of Influence* sets forth Professor Bloom's provocative theory of the literary relationships between the great writers and their predecessors. His most recent books include *Shakespeare: The Invention of the Human,* a 1998 National Book Award finalist; *How to Read and Why; Genius: A Mosaic of One Hundred Exemplary Creative Minds; Hamlet: Poem Unlimited; Where Shall Wisdom Be Found?;* and *Jesus and Yahweh: The Names Divine.* In 1999, Professor Bloom received the prestigious American Academy of Arts and Letters Gold Medal for Criticism. He has also received the International Prize of Catalonia, the Alfonso Reyes Prize of Mexico, and the Hans Christian Andersen Bicentennial Prize of Denmark.

Neil Heims is a freelance writer, editor and researcher. He has a Ph.D in English from the City University of New York. He has written about numerous authors, including John Milton, Arthur Miller, William Shakespeare, Albert Camus, and J.R.R. Tolkien.

John Maynard is Professor of English at New York University. He has been the recipient of a National Endowment for the Humanities Senior Research Grant and a Guggenheim Fellowship. Among his publications are *Browning's Youth; Charlotte Brontë and Sexuality;* and *Victorian Discourses on Sexuality and Religion.*

Irene Tayler is Professor of Literature, Emerita at MIT. Her publications include *Blake's Illustrations to the Poems of Gray* and *Holy Ghosts: The Male Muses of Emily and Charlotte Brontë.*

Anita Levy is an assistant professor of English at the University of Rochester. She is the author of *Other Women: The Writing of Class, Race, and Gender, 1832–1898*, and essays on Emily Brontë, modernism and professionalism, and the formation of the middle class. She is working on a history of middlebrow culture in eighteenth- and nineteenth-century England, provisionally titled "Popular Novel Reading, Sexuality, and the Nation."

John G. Peters teaches English at the University of North Texas. He has written extensively on Joseph Conrad, and his works include *Conrad and Impressionism* and *The Cambridge Introduction to Joseph Conrad*.

Lawrence J. Starzyk is Professor of English at Kent State University. His books include *The Imprisoned Splendor: A Study in Victorian Critical Theory*, *The Dialogue of the Mind with Itself: Early Victorian Poetry and Poetics*, and *If Mine Had Been the Painter's Hand: The Indeterminate in Nineteenth-Century Poetry and Painting*.

Micael M. Clarke is an associate professor of English at Loyala University in Chicago. She is the author of *Thackeray and Women*. Her current projects include a study of Emily Brontë's spiritual and ethical motifs and a study of the university as cultural institution.

Acknowledgments

Maynard, John. *Charlotte Brontë and Sexuality*, 1984, Cambridge University Press. Reprinted with the permission of Cambridge University Press.

Tayler, Irene. *Holy Ghosts: The Male Muses of Emily and Charlotte Brontë*, 1990, Columbia University Press. Reprinted by permission of Columbia University Press.

Levy, Anita. "*Jane Eyre*, the Woman Writer, and the History of Experience." From *Modern Language Quarterly*, Volume 56, no. 1, pp. 77–95. Copyright, 1995, Univeristy of Washington. All rights reserved. Used by permission of the Publisher.

Peters, John G. "Inside and Outside *Jane Eyre* and Marginalization through Labeling." From *Studies in the Novel*, v. 28, no. 1, Spring 1996. Copyright © 1996 by the University of North Texas. Reprinted by permission of the Publisher.

Starzyk, Lawrence J. "The Gallery of Memory: The Pictorial in *Jane Eyre*." From *Papers on Language & Literature*, v. 33, no. 3, Summer 1997. Copyright © The Board of Trustees, Southern Illinois University Edwardsville. Reproduced by permission.

Clarke, Micael M. "Charlotte Brontë's *Jane Eyre* and the Grimms' *Cinderella*." Reprinted, with permission, from SEL *Studies in English Literature* 1500–1900, 4 (Autumn, 2000).

Every effort has been made to contact the owners of copyrighted material and secure copyright permission. Articles appearing in this volume generally appear much as they did in their original publication with few or no editorial changes. In some cases foreign language text has been removed from the original essay. Those interested in locating the original source will find bibliographic information in the bibliography and acknowledgments sections of this volume.

Index

Characters in literary works are indexed by first name (if any), followed by the name of the work in parentheses.